FINDING YOUR VOICE
&
MAKING IT HEARD

BRIA QUINLAN
JEANNIE LIN

LONELY OWL BOOKS

Copyright © 2016 by Bria Quinlan & Jeannie Lin
   All rights reserved.

ISBN-10: 0-9909462-3-1
ISBN-13: 978-0-9909462-3-6

   No part of this book may be reproduced in any form or by any electronic or mechanical means, including information storage and retrieval systems, without written permission from the author, except for the use of brief quotations in a book review.

   Permission Granted for the use of :
   The Chocolate Rose, copyright Laura Florand
   Covert Evidence, copyright Rachel Grant
   Kiss of a Stranger, copyright Lily Dane

TABLE OF CONTENTS

PART I: WHO WE ARE AND WHY WE'RE WRITING THIS BOOK 5

Our Processes 8
How To Use This Book 11
What is Voice and Why Does it Matter? 12

PART II: THINKING ABOUT VOICE 15

The Hierarchy of Voice 15
Style Versus Voice 17
Voice: Your Best Friend or Worst Enemy? 19
One Thing is Not Like the Other 22

PART III: ELEMENTS OF VOICE 27

Why do I need to identify the elements of my Voice? .. 27
Grammar 28
Word Choice 30
Rhythm and Cadence 31
Sentence Structure 32
Pacing 33
Emerging Voice Wrap-Up 34

PART IV: WHERE TO START 36

Approaching Core Voice 36
How We Found Our Voices 37
Finding Your Voice 40
Letting Go of Your Internal Editor 42
Word Choice 43
Strengthening Word Choice 48
Repetition 48

- Onomatopoeic Words 49
- Color Chart – Color Descriptions 50
- Personification 52
- Portmanteau 53
- Anachronisms/Anachronym 53
- Imagery 54
- Simile and Metaphor 56
- Sentence Structure 57
- Cadence 59
- Poetry and Music 60
- Pacing 62
- Adding Dynamic Pacing to Your Scene 63
- Creating Pauses 65

PART V: BEYOND THE BUILDING BLOCKS 68

- Looking Outward 68
- Reading Outside Your Genre 68
- Copy the Greats…Literally 71
- Reading Out Loud: No, Not Your Stuff 73
- Reading Out Loud: Now Your Stuff 74
- Matching the Story 75
- Looking Inward 77
- Amplification 77
- Lazy Description 79
- Maintaining Internal Tension 81
- General strategy 83
- Balance of Dialogue and Narration 86
- Accents, Dialects and Foreign Languages 88
- Layout of Elements 93
- Connotation and Humor 94

    Easing Readers into Your Voice 95
    Identifying Your Fatal Flaws 98

PART VI: ONE VOICE - MULTIPLE VOICES 103

    Multiple Characters, Different Voices 103
    Discovering Your Characters in Pre-Work 104
    D iscovering Your Characters in Re-Work 107
    Secondary Characters 110
    Characters in a Series 112
    So You've Done the Work 114

PART VII: DEVELOPING YOUR SIGNATURE VOICE 118

    Welcome to the Rest of the Battle 118
    Signature Voice: The Game Changer 119
    What Does it Mean to Develop Your Signature Voice? 120
    Identifying Your Sweet Spot 121
    Going Too Far 125
    Get A Little Help 126

PART VIII: VOICE IN PROCESS FOR PANTSERS & PLOTTERS 127

    Holding Onto Your Voice 127
    Inside the Mind of a Pantser 127
    Inside the Mind of a Plotter 131
    Bringing it All Together 136
    Don't Stop Believing! 138

PART IX: APPENDIX A 139

    VOICE AND NARRATIVE POINT OF VIEW 139

PART X: APPENDIX B 147

    Authors & Examples 147

ABOUT THE OWLS 148

PART I

WHO WE ARE AND WHY WE'RE WRITING THIS BOOK

Welcome! If you're picking this book up, it's because you're a writer who has already worked on their basic level of craft. Now you're looking to jump into deeper water and really dig in.

We're Jeannie Lin and Bria Quinlan, and we're thrilled to walk you down that road. Both of us are passionate about writing craft. But how did it all begin?

Lonely Owls refers to the often lonely journey to improving our craft. We found that, while people are constantly talking about the nuts and bolts of the publishing business, we've seen a slow and (to us) sad shift away from discussion about the craft of writing itself. We love craft and we're not ashamed to admit it. We're the Lara Crofts of Craft. It's an adventure and always worth the risk.

But who are we as writers?

BRIA

Everyone's path to publication is different.

I'd gone to school to get a degree in Lit and Creative Writing and a minor in Secondary Education, as well as a copyediting certification from another great school. The goal was—of course—to write. But, after a personal tragedy, my writing was knocked on its butt for years.

It took a long time to start writing for more than just myself. Like any young writer, I was lightly skipping down that path to publishing where everything was new and rosy. I joined local writing groups in an attempt to find critique partners and mentors. It didn't take long to realize that you couldn't just walk in, get accepted, and have the silver bullet handed to you.

It was discouraging (and one of the reasons I still do at least one new writer critique a year). Someone suggested I check out a website called Romance Divas (RD). This was back when online writer groups were mostly still private, cost a lot to join, or had entry qualifications a newbie writer couldn't meet.

RD was a surprise. The group buzzed with talk about craft, had a room for doing writing sprints, hosted monthly workshops, invited newbie questions, and matched writers for critiques.

I met a bunch of writer friends there, including Jeannie Lin.

A few months later, she was in the area for work and asked what she should do with her free night. I jokingly said, Come have dinner with me!

Jeannie is our outgoing Owl. She's an incredible people person with a heart to match, as well as a born marketer. By the time I got her answer, she was in the car.

Dear sweet skies above! Does she not know I'm afraid of people and that was a joke???

This was definitely a surprise for me because I'd never met up with anyone from the internet before, but she seemed (relatively) sane. Little did I know that she would become an amazing friend and partner in writing-crime. After hours of chatter and debate around every craft topic that crossed our minds, we realized we shared a deep passion for not only writing, but writing craft.

Not to mention, we were kicked out of the Cheesecake Factory. Apparently people wanted to go home.

JEANNIE

My path to publication started with an incident while I was teaching high school. One Friday, I broke down crying from the pressure after the students had gone home.

It was the third day of the school year.

Let me tell you, I was no shiny newbie. This was my third year of teaching. But in South Central Los Angeles, we say it's like dog years. I was already considered a veteran.

That weekend, I figured out the problem wasn't my classes or my students or the school. It was me. I needed balance, because it was so easy for teaching to take up every drop of time and blood and sweat. I had always wanted to teach, but there was one other thing I had always wanted to do: write a book.

One of my strengths that I bring to the Owl table is that I have no natural talent for writing. Instead, I'm a perpetual student. I took a class on writing a romance novel and wrote pages on weekends and during spring and summer breaks. I read craft books.

I also joined an online writers' forum called Romance Divas so I could network with other writers. As I hung out there, picking up writing advice and craft tips along the way, I started seeing a certain Bria Quinlan showing up in the same threads I frequented. One day, the opportunity came to meet face-to-face.

By the way, let it be known that I'm not necessarily the outgoing Owl. I just have poor impulse control and perpetual wandering feet. Driving for hours to hook up and talk about writing seemed like a great idea! As our Lonely Owl moniker implies, writing is often a lonely endeavor. It's in my nature to seek out others with the same geeky tendencies. Owls of a feather and all.

Eventually I finished my first manuscript and started the cycle of querying and submitting and contest stalking. I latched on to RWA's Golden Heart® contest as a way to get my writing out there.

Bria, ever the ringleader, asked on Romance Divas if anyone wanted to exchange pages for the contest. Neither of us finaled that year, but something even better happened. It was the start of a beautiful relationship. We stayed together as critique partners through our first published books and the ones that came after. We grew together as our careers developed and the industry changed. At the heart of it, we were still crafters, looking hard at what we were doing as well as the books we read in order to figure out what was working or not working.

Fast forward to Penned Con 2014...

We roomed together for the conference and sat up late one night, doing our standard craft nerd gabbing. Our reader friend Angie Hulsman (Unsuspected Bookworm) listened to all of this and told us, "You guys should teach a class."

Lightbulb moment!

Two former teachers with writing and editing experience and a passion for craft? We should teach a class...which we did. Which led to this book and the Lonely Owls craft brand.

Thank you, Angie!

OUR PROCESSES

Throughout the book we'll discuss how we hone our voices inside each of our processes for each project. Because of this, we want to start out with a brief description of those processes. We'll keep it simple, since that could be an entire book within itself. These are ten-thousand-foot views of our individual approaches to help you picture some of the examples we'll discuss later.

If you've spent any time around writers, you've heard the general terms Plotting and Pantsing, two sides of the writing process.

Plotters plan out their character and story events, i.e., they work out a plot prior to sitting down to write the story. Pantsers are said to "fly by the seat of their pants" and do not lay out a specific sequence of story events ahead of time.

Rather than being a hard line in the sand, it's really a sliding scale that gives authors a template for discussing writing approach and process.

Picture a line that fades from white down to gray, then back out to black.

The middle ground covers an area some people would call dark and some would call light. The ends are more defined.

That's the type of spectrum we're talking about.

Zero planningIntensive Pre-planning
No pre-determined plotStep by step plot outline
No storyboards or mapsCreate storyboards or maps
Discover characters while writingCharacter sketches

BRIA

On the scale of Plotter to Pantser, I'm on the far end of Pantser. One thing people may not realize is there are a lot of different ways to be a Pantser. But today we're just going to look at my overall process.

My first step is getting to know my character, premise, and black moment (the All Is Lost moment). Those three things typically come to me at the same time. Once I let them play in my head, I sit down to write the Disaster Draft.

Long before I'd heard of Candace Haven's Fast Drafting method (FD), I pretty much wrote the way she teaches. Finding FD gave me a framework for talking about my process that people had heard of and understood. It also meant other writers stopped telling me I was nuts, because someone had made this a more valid way to finish your first draft.

Of course, as you saw above, I can't even call it a first draft. The point—for me—is to rush through getting the story on the page, identifying the blind spots I had going in, and letting go of any idea of starting near "good enough." I don't stop for anything. There are notes and lists and commentary as much as there are narrative and dialogue. This isn't about anything but getting it out.

I then do a read-through (a pass through a book, looking at certain aspects of it). At this point I make a list of everything I need to revise, consider, add, or research. I make as many changes during the actual read-through process as possible. Now I have a first draft.

The next step is creating my revision cards. Using my own read-through and a list of things to look out for, I search for patterns and themes, then combine these into revision cards to work through. It keeps me focused on the issues and moving forward. I rework the book to where I think it needs to be. This is a big process. This isn't a "do it all as I read through the book one more time" thing. Sometimes it's spot work. Sometimes it's an entire pass.

Then I let it sit. Repeat once. After this round, usually it's off to the critique partners and/or beta readers.

And then…hopefully…I'll fix the things they suggest and polish. After that, it's time for the editor.

Oh, if only it were truly as simple as that sounds!

JEANNIE

I fall into the Plotter side of the scale, where I plan out turning points and key moments of the story before I start writing. There are many different ways to be a Plotter, with varying degrees of planning and outlining. I consider myself a moderate Plotter in that I put a skeleton outline in place so I know where I'm going, but I leave a lot of the discovery to the actual drafting process. I'm also an incubator. I will hold on to an idea for a while and let it germinate before even starting to lay down plot.

In my ideal process, I begin with a kernel of a story idea that I'll take into the brainstorming phase. During this initial process, I identify themes the story will revolve around. It's a semi-organic process. Writers have themes they return to again and again, subconsciously or consciously. These are the muses that form our points of view. These core themes feed our unique voices—but more on this later! I'm getting ahead of myself.

The key factor for me is that I have an idea of the larger themes of the story before I start writing. When I plot, I have an overarching idea or ideas that guide where I lead my characters.

The first thing I'll put down on paper is an outline. I started out as a short story writer, so when I switched to writing novels, I had a huge issue with pacing. I picked up the habit of following the standard three-act structure (or the "Six Stage Plot Structure" as described by Michael Hauge) in order to lay out the plot.

After outlining and incubating, I write an ugly draft full of holes and gaps, but I write from start to finish. Then I run through to fill in the gaps and create what I call a human consumable draft. At this point, I hand it off to a few trusted readers.

From their critiques and comments as well as my own thoughts, I put together a "revision letter" for myself, highlighting what I want to target during revision. Depending on how deep the edits are, I may split the passes up with one main goal per pass: hero's motivation, increasing conflict, etc.

For me, the true crafting of the story happens during revisions. I'm one of those writers who finds drafting a painful and angst-ridden time during which I lose all faith that life will ever be good again. I'm not joking, Bria can attest to that. (Bria here: attesting!) With revisions, I have a defined goal and a set of problems to solve and all is well.

I often wonder what my betas must think of me as a writer. There is a drastic difference between the last draft anyone sees and the final version that hits my editor. Only when all the structural story issues have been resolved do I feel comfortable enough to polish and edit for Voice.

HOW TO USE THIS BOOK

Both Owls come from an education background. With that in mind, we've formalized a learning journey that can be individualized.

This isn't a "sit down and read it in one sitting" type of book. We've created a framework and exercises to help you drill down to the heart of your voice, absorb your own gifts, and expand on them. Get ready to be really hands-on with your work!

We're coming at this with the assumption you've already done other craft work. While Voice is an incredibly interesting topic, it's not a light and fluffy place to start. With that, we're also assuming you already have some written pieces to work with. If not, this might be a book you want to put away until you have begun work on your first manuscript.

We're going to get our hands dirty. You're going to need some materials to keep track of your work, so grab your manuscript and a notebook.

We highly recommend keeping the original version of your manuscript out as you edit and revise so you can see where you started. There will be gems in there you want to keep that you may not spot until you're nearing the end of the journey. Save those. The goal is to learn to dig deep without over-editing.

So get ready to dive in and bring your writing voice to the next level!

NOTE: We're going to reference a lot of authors and books here. There's a list of references in the appendix.

WHAT IS VOICE AND WHY DOES IT MATTER?

We've all read books we've enjoyed, maybe even loved as far as the story went, but nothing about the book stood out to us when we think back on it. Our job as authors is to get beyond that. We want our work to be more than a moment's enjoyment.

Author Voice plays a huge part in that.

If you ask most writers what their Author Voice is, they'll often tell you something like, "I have a humorous voice" or "I have a lyrical voice." But that's actually just a shorthand description and the tip of the iceberg. It's like when we say "popular jock" or "dorky computer guy." These are shorthand descriptions that refer to stereotypes. Stereotypes may have some basis in reality, but aren't actually true descriptions of an entire group.

Take, for example, our "dorky computer guy." This stereotype assumes that everyone who successfully works with computers is male. It also assumes we all have the same definition of "dorky." Obviously we don't. There are connotations attached to the word, but even those will differ. Or, if someone is wearing glasses, they must be incredibly intelligent...and dorky. (One Owl feels particularly annoyed by this example.) When someone says "funny voice," it leaves us with the same problem. Your humor and my humor may differ greatly.

Because Voice is difficult to define and elusive to grasp, it often leaves even seasoned authors feeling at a loss. Your voice and craft deserve more attention than shortcuts and stereotypes. A stereotype is seldom a source of power.

To harness the power of Voice, you need to push further than a generic description of your own. Why does it matter if you're able to define a particular author's voice? Or, more importantly, if you can define your own voice?

Defining your voice allows you to pinpoint usable aspects. This is the first step to being able to utilize Voice in the most effective ways. Describing one feature of your voice, like above, is a great way to start. But it doesn't encompass or account for the full magnitude of a well-oiled voice.

This means going on a journey to not only enrich your voice but to draw upon your newly acquired knowledge to push your writing to its full potential. We want each of you to broaden your understanding of Voice, find its furthest boundaries, and then focus back in to finding your own signature voice.

There are several things we'll be working on to accomplish this:
- Defining Voice and its hierarchy of layers
- Deconstructing the building blocks of a strong voice using examples
- Developing your unique voice for maximum effect

Just like any journey to self-discovery, ours will take hard work and scrutiny. But don't worry! We're here to make it fun as well as informative.

Story is what the reader is initially aware of, but Voice is the key to creating an unforgettable reading experience. Without a clear Voice, the story is in danger of being lost. Even the most exciting adventure can become dull in the execution.

Let's take the first step today!

PART II

THINKING ABOUT VOICE

THE HIERARCHY OF VOICE

In our years of studying craft, we were both often frustrated with the elusive definitions and discussions around Voice.

We're always trying to put our fingers on what makes our favorite reads so powerful.

After looking at our own writing, and that of our favorite authors, we brought certain assertions to our critiquing and editing that allowed us to formulate a framework to approach and hone Voice—both in our own writing and when working with others.

It became clear to us that all writing could be split into three levels: Emerging, Core, and Signature Voices.

In this book, we're going to discuss the definitions of each level and how to progress through and beyond each level to reach the peak of your craft. Remember, no one thing will be the magic bullet for Voice. But working through the building blocks and the corresponding exercises, each of you will climb the levels as you discover your strengths and how your own work fits into that.

For now, let's look at the basic definitions of the three levels of our Voice Hierarchy.

EMERGING VOICE

This is where all writers start. This is a necessary step and should be where the exciting experimentation begins. Usually we find ourselves putting words together that sound good to our untrained ears. Often we begin the learning process through imitation of things we respect and admire. Another first attempt at honing your Voice could lead to overworking the draft. Or Voice may not be on your radar, so it isn't being crafted yet at this point.

Your Emerging Voice is dominant at this stage in your writing craft.

CORE VOICE

This is the Voice level that is distinctly yours. Once you find it, it's going to stay with you as the basis of your work through your career. Here is where you've taken your experiments and sharpened them into something that flows more naturally. Most of the work for our journey together will be reaching for and honing this Core Voice.

SIGNATURE VOICE

Your Signature Voice is the final, most specific level. This is how you use your Core Voice. This type goes beyond the basics to take your Core Voice and build upon it to construct an elevated Voice that is part of your story, brand, and author identity. Authors who have harnessed their Core Voice and have focused it into a branded Signature Voice are the ones who make an impact on their readers. These authors have voices that are immediately identifiable from small snippets and have achieved that special something that readers seek out because they can't find it anywhere else.

This is our goal for you: to develop your Core Voice and build up your writer's toolbox. Once there, you'll move on to exploring and refining your Signature Voice with a solid foundation to build on. Your "voice work" becomes more focused and targeted as you pinpoint what uniquely makes you a standout voice in the crowd.

Every writer will have exciting times of growth, comfortable plateaus, challenging struggles, and moments of brilliance. If you're serious about bettering your craft, you'll understand that growing and getting better is a continuous effort—not only because self-improvement is a lifelong journey, but because writing and publishing keep changing as well.

With that in mind, this book will provide a guide as well as leave you with tools that will sustain your future efforts. At the end of our material, you will understand Emerging Voice (which we'll be referring to as simply Voice from now on), discover your Core Voice, and begin shaping your Signature Voice for the greatest impact.

STYLE VERSUS VOICE

Often when we talk about voice we partner it with discussions about style.

This can be confusing because so often the words are erroneously used interchangeably. It's easy to see how this could happen since style is a familiar word. We talk about style in so many parts of our lives: clothing, décor, how we live our lives. Style isn't a word we struggle with. It's a comfortable place.

But style is not voice.

Style is the surface manifestation of Voice. It's the pretty exterior that lies over the sturdy construct of Voice beneath it.

Let's pretend! Let's say that your manuscript is a nice, comfortable house constructed and decorated exactly how you want it to be.

Voice is the foundation of that house, the frame and studs and drywall.

Style is the layout and the color you paint on that drywall and even the paintings you hang on the walls.

Together these two elements create a rich environment, built from the ground up. How does style fit into the Voice hierarchy?

Style is what readers see or sense on the surface. It is their initial impression.

Voice, however, is all the elements a casual observer doesn't notice: the combination, the balance, and the composition of all the components that are essential to how the entire look comes together. It goes down to what specific accessories were chosen and the quality of the items.

Let's try this: picture dressing for a big event. (Gentlemen, bear with us. You'll get the point even with dresses as our example. We promise.)

Style in the first level (Voice) would be like going into the store and telling the salesgirl you want a black, knee-length dress with short sleeves, letting her bring you one, and then buying it.

Style on the second level (Core Voice) would mean picking out a dress that is exactly what you want. It has lace across the top, with little cap sleeves and a flounce hem that flips exactly how you want it to when you walk. When your friends see it, they say, "Oh that's so you."

But what about Signature Voice? What could the third level bring that isn't covered in that Core Voice level?

Style at the third level would be getting that perfect dress, then finding something unique as an accessory. Something no one else would pair with the perfect dress. Something that makes people think of you.

It's not just that the "dress is so you," but that you've brought something together that would make people think of you even if they saw it in the store without you. It's that pin no one else would buy, but you rock it. That special way you do your hair that would look crazy on someone else, but looks stylish and fun on you. And not only does it look perfect on you, but you are the one known for creating that look and making it a "thing."

VOICE: YOUR BEST FRIEND OR WORST ENEMY?

And the answer is...both.

Finding the right way to utilize your voice will bring you to a better place as an author. But finding your voice doesn't mean all your problems are solved. Both of us found out the hard way that Voice can be your best friend...or your worst enemy.

Once we both found our voices, we were fairly quick in getting agents and heading out on submissions. And that's where the next Voice barrier appeared.

BRIA

For me, my voice was my worst enemy with editors. Teen issue books by a writer with a background of working with teens and that have a romance? GREAT!

Unfortunately, every time we had editorial interest, the answer came back, "What is this? It's funny? Issue books aren't funny. Where would we shelve this?"

That last question always seemed annoyingly amusing since at the time YA was still just one shelf that said YOUNG ADULT. I finally strongly suggested to my long-suffering agent that we tell them to just "freaking put it under 'Q' and be done with it."

Long-Suffering Agent said this might not help us win friends and influence people.

After a particularly stupid rejection, I called Long-Suffering Agent. She answered the phone with, "We're pulling everything and you're self-publishing, right?"

Yes. That's what happened. Now the market gets that not all teens deal with issues by going dark and are looking for more books like mine.

Sometimes it's not your voice. It's your timing.

JEANNIE

For me, my voice was absolutely my best friend, guardian angel, and fairy godmother—or rather it helped me find my fairy godmother.

When I was starting out, everyone used to say that editors were looking for a great Voice. If you have a great Voice, readers will follow you. Voice. Voice. Voice.

I had no idea what that meant.

I also had no idea that no one was looking for a Chinese historical romance set in the eighth century with elements of martial arts drama.

The problem was that as soon as I finished and started querying, it became very clear I had a manuscript that was a very hard sell. But I was still so shiny that I couldn't be discouraged. Sure, there wasn't really anything like this out there...but what if? What if I could convince them this was exactly what they wanted?

I went through close to a hundred rejections, never even scratching the surface. A few partial requests turned into requests for the complete manuscript, but the rejections always came back with, "Interesting story, but not quite right."

I knew something was missing. I knew I didn't have that It Factor, because people were not finishing the book. So I kept at it, trying everything under the sun (I was living in my Emerging Voice period).

The first time an agent called to offer representation, she told me, "You have a voice."

That word again.

A few days later, another agent called. "Every editor out there is hoping to find the new Voice in romance. When I read this, I thought, this is it. This is the new Voice."

I sat there, blinking and stunned.

This was a historical romance between a Chinese princess and a Western barbarian set in the Tang Dynasty with sword fights. No one in the romance industry was looking for this book. No one even knew something like this existed.

But something had changed. I had gone from a year of hearing nothing but "No" to "Your voice is going to sell this."
And it did.

ONE THING IS NOT LIKE THE OTHER

One thing we've found when discussing Voice with newer writers is that they're far too close to their own writing to be able to hear their own voice.

Hand them a book by someone they idolize and, of course, they know they'd love to write like that. But ask them what makes that specific author's voice strong and unique, and they lose the ability to define the nuts and bolts of it.

At first glance, something like "rich description" might be a good place to start. And it is, but it's also a ten-thousand-foot view.

Let's dive in and look at some examples to clarify. Here's a sample of a descriptive passage from Lily Dane's *Kiss of a Stranger*:

> *The town's sign was rough and weathered, its edges warped. It wasn't one of those new modern signs with laser-printed white letters. This was aged wood, the once rich cedar now a dull gray. The letters were burned into the surface and coated with paint, most of which had faded long ago.*
>
> *Welcome to Lost Coast Harbor, it said.*
>
> *Gabe's tight-lipped smile was brutal as he stepped across the town line. For six years, he'd pored over maps, memorizing the names of every street, from the main highway to the smallest alley. He didn't hesitate when he hit first one fork in the road, then another.*
>
> *Whoever named the town hadn't been joking. The town wasn't in the middle of nowhere. It was on the very edge of nowhere, pressed up against the enormous swell of the Pacific Ocean. It perched on the ragged cliffs of the Northern California coast, as though it hadn't quite decided whether or not to jump into the churning water below.*

The passage begins with details before transitioning into character development and introspection. The sentences during the initial observation and subsequent introspection are directly stated.

And now take a look at Rachel Grant's *Covert Evidence*:

> *A drink would dampen his reflexes, and he needed to stay on guard. He poured a splash of scotch into a glass. A taste. That was all he could have.*
>
> *Story of his life.*
>
> *He could view, and at times even sample, the pleasures other men took for granted, but the comforts of American life weren't for him. He'd given his life over to his country, and lived—and deep down believed he'd someday die—for that service. When he finished a job, he moved to the next one, never pausing to enjoy the very liberty he sacrificed for.*
>
> *He replaced the stopper and turned to face the balcony, avoiding Zack's interested gaze for the moment. Ian had known Zack was listening to every moment of his "date" with Cressida. It was necessary and expedient that his backup on this op be fully informed.*
>
> *But that didn't mean he liked it. The idea of Cressida's vulnerable flirtation being witnessed, even mocked, by another agent left a bitter taste in his mouth that even the scotch couldn't burn away.*
>
> *Lake Van glistened in the darkness beyond the window. Something about this sleepy, underdeveloped part of Turkey called to him, but was another pleasure he could sample but never fully enjoy.*
>
> *As was the woman he would tail for the next few days.*

> *If he were Hindu, he'd wonder who he'd pissed off in a previous life to find himself in this situation. But he wasn't Hindu. He wasn't Muslim. He was a secular warrior in the midst of a holy war, and his primary goal was to protect his country from being targeted or drawn into the battle.*

    The passage opens immediately with the narrator's state of mind. Grant's sentences draw out longer, bringing more of the hero's emotions into view.

    Both of these are descriptions of a place seen through the male lead's eyes.

    The best part of each of these passages is that they tell us not just where he is and what he thinks of the place, but something about him.

    Both passages move beyond a basic description. They both use details in a way that marks the character even more than the setting.

    Both are examples of rich description. Both are distinctive voices. The problem is, they're nothing alike. Saying "rich description" doesn't tell us about Voice as much as it informs on the style being used.

    Both get us to a great understanding of where we are and what the hero is thinking and feeling, but with such different voice, style, pace, tone, and word choice that you'd never confuse one for the other.

    If I asked you explain the passages to me in five words or less, I'm betting those five words would be a variation of the following: descriptive introductory passage, male POV.

    So let's move up a step. Away from the overview of these two vivid descriptions and see how to build beyond that five-word tip of the iceberg. At the Core Voice stage, you might say, "Bria writes light and fluid description, and Jeannie writes rich, story-expanding description." This is slightly better. Moving away from genre classifications as a way of defining your voice allows you to attack

Voice from as many angles as possible. It's like seeing a prism with the light coming in from another side. Keep taking steps around it and you'll eventually get the whole picture.

To find another way to look at things, let's put a new spin on this. Let's move away from books to music and use a different part of our creative minds.

Everyone has heard a Frank Sinatra song or two. There are many imitators and too many replicators, but there's only one Ol' Blue Eyes. The tone, cadence, word choice and play, how he uses the band...Everything about his technique beyond the physical sound of his voice is the Signature Voice of his music.

He was a pro at playing with all the elements to accentuate each one and hold tight to his listeners. Love him or hate him, there's a flavor to his work that makes it clear it's him each and every time. He was so in touch with "his thing" that he reached the ultimate artistic goal: making it look easy. You know when you hear him.

Not a music person? That's okay. Let's look at movies. Authors love to look at movies, right?

Director Baz Luhrmann (Romeo + Juliet, Strictly Ballroom, Moulin Rouge) has a directorial approach that's incredibly easy to identify. If he were an author, we'd look at that as his voice. You open to any page (or any shot, in this example), and you know you're looking at a Baz picture. The texture, the angles, the use of light and color, the whimsicalness of handling even the ugliest things.

Spielberg, Lucas, Ephron, whoever...Pick another famous director. They would each take the same script and turn it into a completely different movie. You'd know it was their work.

Imagine if Michael Bay directed Star Wars. First off, there'd be even more explosions. Instead of the plot pushing the action, the action would push (or drag) the plot. Ah-ha moments would happen during huge sequences instead of those subtle, quiet moments that Lucas found inside the action.

Same story, plot, characters, and script, directed by famous, talented people in the same subgenre (action)...different Voice.

Below is the first of many Brain Flexes throughout the book. Each exercise is built specifically for that section, but usually the work we do there will be built upon in future chapters.

BRAIN FLEX

Identify three writers you love who have distinctive voices.

What are the qualities that make them different from one another? What feelings do those differences leave you with as a reader? When you think of their author voice, what emotional response do you have?

CHECK IN

Now you have a baseline for your views on Voice. Remember, we're not looking to copy or mimic—but we do want to have a collection of works to learn from.

Keep that list nearby for easy reference. You'll want to refer to it later.

PART III

ELEMENTS OF VOICE

As you can guess, there's a lot going on when considering Voice.

At the Emerging Voice level, we're examining many different components while we experiment. The goal here for you is to look deeper into your own writing and find what makes you and your approach different from anyone else.

WHY DO I NEED TO IDENTIFY THE ELEMENTS OF MY VOICE?

If you're reading this book, you're like us. You're looking for the tools and techniques to make a conscious effort to improve your writing. To do this, you first need to focus on the root elements that form the building blocks of craft.

No great artist can generate masterpieces without first understanding the components of their building materials. Those building materials are the smallest, simplest elements of the book you're working on. We need to understand the components that make up good writing so we have a basis for exploring ways to improve, as well as having a common language for discussing these developments.

There is no accidental improvement of craft. Without understanding what builds a good Voice, you can't focus your efforts to get there.

To that point, we're going to look at the base level of the Elements of Voice that we work with when we're in the Emerging section of the Voice Hierarchy.

Before developing a Core Voice, we had to identify what we considered our Emerging Voice. And that process took a lot of experimentation. It took many drafts and revision notes. In Bria's case, it took trying out a new genre. In Jeannie's case, it required getting feedback from a gazillion contests and trying different approaches.

The path toward finding your Core Voice and subsequently developing your Signature Voice will not be the same for everyone. One of the major milestones in developing your voice is knowing what you want that voice to be. Each writer sets their own goals at each step.

In truth, this is a two-part process. You are both examining your writing to assess how you currently write and pushing yourself beyond your boundaries to identify what you're striving for.

Knowing what the elements of Voice are is key to applying the right tool at the right time. We've identified some major elements that are the building blocks of Voice. Understanding them allows you to play with each in different ways at different times. This also provides a basis for our discussion and exercises.

Here we're going to provide an overview of the elements from the perspective of an Emerging Level Voice. We'll dive deeper into each element and expand upon them later in the book.

These elements include grammar, word choice, sentence structure and pacing, and rhythm and cadence.

GRAMMAR

There. We said it. We strongly believe it's not a four-letter word. For one reason, because we can count. For another because it's your best friend, your most critical tool, and the foundation for the rest of your Voice work.

Let's start with what grammar is. Grammar is the way we put together sentences in our language. It's the proper use of words, the connection of verbs and nouns, and the matching of objects, pronouns, adverbs, and adjectives.

We see that face you're making. That's a lot of grammar.

But the best part is, most of us already know the basics. It just comes down to making sure that we're following the rules in a way that makes our writing clear.

The tricky thing about grammar is that it is invisible if it's doing its job. You never think about grammar unless there's a flaw in it, much like the foundation of your house. Once you discover there's an issue, it becomes the number one repair priority or the house is worthless.

If your grasp of grammar isn't solid, readers won't be able to see beyond the flaws, making your voice and storytelling ability moot.

We already know what you're about to say. Whatever your reason is, whoever you're pointing at as an example of why you don't need to play by the rules, that's all well and good. Sometimes it's even correct.

There's an often-quoted, widely acknowledged truth (although often not widely enough) in the Romance world: You're not Nora.

Internationally Best-Selling Author Nora Roberts is a pro with decades of hard work and experience under her belt. When she breaks a rule, she breaks it knowing fully well why she's doing it.

When we see the biggest and brightest authors doing things in their books that are bad grammar or poor writing practices, we often use it as an excuse to write in a similar fashion.

It must not be important to follow this grammar rule because so-and-so doesn't follow it. Only, as stated above, you're not so-and-so. You may be one day, but most of us won't be. And that's okay!

Here is the Owl Rule for Breaking Rules: If you break it, break it with purpose.

Not on purpose—with purpose.

To do that, you need to have a strong grasp of grammar and all its elements.

This isn't a grammar book. There are some great free grammar tools out there on this little hidden device we've found called the internet. A quick brush up on the basics is a great place to start.

WORD CHOICE

Word choice is exactly what it sounds like: The specific words the author has selected for the purpose of communication. At the Emerging Voice phase, this might be done without too much thought. We're getting the words down on the page and finding our flow.

As we continue to write and reread/rework our manuscripts, we find patterns and habits and words that are overused. To correct them, we then go to the extreme in the other direction. Often the overwhelming urge is to revise and polish to improve word usage.

These are both natural stages in Voice development. The Emerging phase isn't the time to beat ourselves up over word choice. One thing a lot of us realize coming out of the Emerging phase is that it's probably time to put the thesaurus away. At this level, our job, when it comes to word choice, is awareness. To become aware of what words we use, how often we use them, and how we use them.

So, you've come this far and you're ready to start working on your own stuff. Word choice! Yes! Something you can play with...but how?

Here's a chance to take a breath and apply what you just learned to your own work.

Don't get stuck here, but don't breeze by these. Even seasoned writers need a review now and then.

BRAIN FLEX

Looking to get a good feel about word choice at the Emerging level? Pick three pages from your current work in progress for a read-through. Highlight words you don't use in everyday language or that stand out to you when you read them aloud.

This is also a good time to highlight the hero and/or heroine's names to see if you're in the habit of relying too heavily on proper name usage.

Circle any words that stand out as repetitive—usually we call this echoing.

Did any words make you pause upon rereading? Did you find any comfort or go-to words that you used repeatedly? Did you see the hero or heroine's name echoing over and over? On the flip side, was there a sea of pronouns such as "he" and "she" or "I"?

CHECK IN

Though you may feel the urge to revise, don't go and "fix" any of this now. The goal is to learn about your tendencies. Some of these habits may turn out to be fine, or they may even end up being key to your personal voice.

Remember, for things like word choice, every manuscript will differ.

You've probably heard authors talking about "this book's word." What they mean is the word they've used as a crutch for that book. Words like "just" or "very" that act as weak modifiers often fall into this group.

RHYTHM AND CADENCE

Rhythm and cadence are partners in crime—so they're usually referenced together. Collectively they are the flow of your words, the pattern they set up auditorily to your inner ear.

The easiest way to experience the rhythm and cadence of your writing or any writing is to read it out loud and pay attention to the rise and fall of the words and sentences. Does the writing flow well? Move quickly? Or is the rhythm choppy, with many short sentences and phrases? At this first level, don't worry about how you're using the techniques to tell the story. This is the time to become aware of your own natural patterns and decide if they are working or not.

BRAIN FLEX

Wondering how to spot rhythm and cadence?

Rhythm and cadence become more obvious when you read authors who are known for it. Grab a sample of someone like Frank McCourt, Stephen King, or Cormac McCarthy. All three of these authors are known for the distinctive way their passages ebb and flow. Read it out loud and watch yourself naturally fall into the pattern they set for their readers.

CHECK IN

Did you find a comfortable flow in the words? Did it feel natural? How did it impact the way you felt about the story—or how did the rhythm dictate the way you read it?

These authors are known for their cadence. It's clear and part of their Voice *and* brand.

Not every Voice needs to have a cadence that is so clearly identifiable, but understanding the power of cadence and rhythm can help you to harness it when you need it.

SENTENCE STRUCTURE

What does sentence structure at the Emerging level look like? In a word: repetition.

Some of the tendencies of the Emerging Voice:

- Starting every sentence with a basic noun/verb combination
- Frequently beginning sentences with similar phrases
- Relying on long compound sentences

We tend to fall into a comfortable pattern of our own making. Not only is this not a surprise at this level, it actually makes perfect sense! We're working on getting words out. On putting the story on the page. This is how it should be!

BRAIN FLEX

Curious how diverse your sentence structures are? There's a quick and easy way to eyeball if there's much difference overall.

Pick a page and highlight every other sentence. This will let you spot the length of each pretty quickly.

Are the sentences different or do they all look the same? If the lengths are almost all identical, then your writing is naturally falling into a pattern where each line is similar.

CHECK IN

Hopefully you saw different patterns based on pace, dialogue, prose, etc. Using the knowledge of your structure is a great way to tighten, speed up, slow down, and emphasize important sections.

This is an excellent exercise to use on all your turning points.

PACING

For an Emerging Voice, pacing is nothing more complicated than how quickly your story moves. Is the story progressing quickly or slowly? While it feels obvious that a story moving too slowly is a place for improvement, a story can also move too fast.

Elements like sentence structure can contribute to pacing, but we separated it out into its own section. This is how readers usually register the effect of the other elements. For instance, constant hiccups in grammar will slow a read. A sentence structure of many short, rapid-fire sentences may make a read feel fast-paced.

Pacing is about striking a proper balance that matches the rising and falling tension in the story. It's quite complicated when you think about it. You also can't judge pace by just reading through one scene at a time.

At the Emerging Voice level, we haven't had a lot of experience thinking of the manuscript as a whole. For example, it's quite common to write one scene at a time, one chapter at a time. Then we feed these scenes to critique partners the same way, bit by bit as our story unfolds. Pacing is something we will work on more in-depth as all the other pieces start coming together.

At the Emerging level, the best indicator of pace is to have someone read your work. It's important that they actually read enough of the work, spanning several contiguous chapters, in order to gauge pacing.

EMERGING VOICE WRAP-UP

This was either a good starting point for you or a review of the basics. Often, as writers, we jump into writing far ahead of our skill level. Writing is something we do daily, and it feels like these components should come as naturally as speech.

There's a distinct difference between daily communications and the complex art of storytelling with a fully engaged Voice.

Now that we've laid the flagstone level basics down in our story yard, we're going to move forward, climbing the slope to identifying and developing Core Voice.

As you move beyond the initial Emerging phase, and you've finished a manuscript or two, it's natural to realize you need to revise and polish. At that point, it's also natural to seek feedback and reread your own work.

In that cycle, most of us will hit a roadblock where we want to bring our work to the next level, but we don't know how. We may start getting a flood of feedback, all saying different things and pointing us in different directions. We don't know which piece of advice to take and usually the feedback can't pinpoint where and how we need to improve either. As they say, if this was easy, everyone would do it, right?

When we haven't examined our writing deeply, we're blind to the flagstones we're missing. On the other hand, we may also be overusing or overworking these basic components.

The next slope will give us a better view of these techniques as they pertain to our writing. Then we can better utilize them.

The key to the process is to take a long, hard look at your writing with the intent of forming a plan to move toward a truly distinctive voice. This is where the hard work (and the fun part) really kicks in.

But what does distinctive truly mean?

Isn't every voice naturally unique?

Well, we're going to dispense with the warm and fuzzies here and say no. Your voice is not naturally unique. Or rather, it's not unusual enough for readers to take note.

If we refer to the levels of voice development, your Emerging Voice is the first level, your starting point. There are some personal preferences inherently in there, such as your own use of techniques and devices. This Voice is where we live. It's our natural communication style. We have intrinsic strengths that we've probably leaned on heavily here, but it's time to start incorporating the full complement of techniques to craft a Voice that builds into something beyond our baseline style.

Our goal is to start both defining and building on our strengths as well as identifying our as-yet undeveloped or underdeveloped tools in the course of finding our Core Voice. Here you will focus on reshaping your voice into something more deliberate. The goal isn't to scrap what you do, but to make you into a better you.

This is not to say that a great Voice is flowery or descriptive. Nor does it mean the ideal Voice is super-polished or sparse. Your Voice is the one unique It Factor you bring to the table. It's the way you tell a story that's different from anyone else regardless of the plot, subject matter, and setting. A distinctive voice means the reader can only get that added special flavor and perspective from one place—and that's from you.

Distinctive Voices are memorable voices.

PART IV

WHERE TO START

APPROACHING CORE VOICE

Your Core Voice has a sense of itself and what it's trying to accomplish. Finding your Core Voice isn't the end of the journey, but it's certainly a major milestone in discovering who you want to be as a writer. At least it was for us Owls.

We've mentioned before that Voice is one of those nebulous things that's hard to put your finger on. For this reason, it can feel strange and forced to have to think so consciously about your writing. Plus, a lot of the joy of writing comes from just letting things flow and seeing what comes out!

In fact, when we were brainstorming what material to include in our Voice discussion and exercises, we had to stop and consciously dig up ideas we had internalized over the years. These tips and techniques are our way of taking a step back, visualizing, and breaking down how we've evolved as writers and turning that information into teachable units.

We're not saying analytical process is something we engage in on a daily basis, nor is it something we advocate you do all the time. The goal is for you to reach a point where you can write naturally and what comes out is a more focused and distinctive version of you.

This section is a collection of different approaches and exercises to stimulate your writing brain. Some of the techniques may ring more true to you than others, but the intent is to give you many choices to spark your creativity.

HOW WE FOUND OUR VOICES

You may not recognize right away when you've found your voice. There will come a day when the writing seems to flow a bit more easily, when you find yourself struggling a bit less over word choice or cadence or timing. Content is still content, but now your approach has shifted to be more heavily focused on what to say and shifting away from how to say it.

Most people don't wake up one day and say, Eureka! I found my voice.

For both of us, finding our Core Voice was a surprise. We knew something was different, but we didn't know it was the slow, struggling slip into Voice until the other pointed it out.

JEANNIE'S STORY

I was at the point where my beta readers and critique groups were all saying, "It's good. It's good." But it obviously wasn't good enough because agents and editors kept passing without so much as a moment's pause. I was determined to figure out what I needed to do to improve. I started entering contests to get opinions from people who didn't love me. Highly recommended: get opinions from people who do not love you.

After getting feedback, I'd tweak and polish. And resubmit. And query another set of agents. And enter more contests.

It reached the point where I felt I'd polished the life out of my story. I was trying to fix all the flaws that readers had pointed out, and the writing had become controlled and stiff as a result. It felt as if I absolutely would never, ever break through. This thing had been rewritten to death.

At that time, I was reading a lot of first books. I like the rawness and freshness of first books. There may be rough spots, but there are some sparkly moments because the authors aren't seasoned and established and perfect.

One of the books that stuck with me was Joanna Bourne's *Spymaster's Lady*. Bourne's writing was so bold. Her prose had so many little quirks and twists and habits that were uniquely hers. The writing wasn't perfectly polished and safe. It took risks.

I had finished my second manuscript at that time, and immediately started writing my third book, *The Dragon and the Pearl*. At the same time, I went back and started revising my second manuscript for the hundredth time.

But this time I was no longer trying to polish. This time I decided to stop trying to do things right and make mistakes instead—my very own beautiful mistakes.

And then I started the cycle of submitting to contests and querying agents all over again.

From the moment I made a concerted effort to amplify my writing, people started noticing. Every single contest I entered after this point, I finaled in. I started getting more requests from agents. I started getting actual feedback in my rejection letters. Something had changed. The change seemed so minor to me, but it was noticeable to readers.

What exactly had happened? I didn't put my finger exactly on it until Bria did a read-through of *The Dragon and the Pearl*.

"This is four times the book *Butterfly Swords* is," she told me. "You've found your voice."

BRIA

There was such a resounding click when I read *The Dragon and the Pearl* for the first time. It wasn't error-free, and Jeannie still had draft things to work on like all books have at that point. But they actually felt lighter because of the beauty of reading a story with such a powerful, natural Voice.

I knew by page three that the game had just 100% changed.

BRIA'S STORY

My first manuscript was also my first love: YA Fantasy.

Back then, I'd been told right away it was going to be a nearly impossible sell. It was definitely for younger teen girls. Sounds like a good idea…now.

In retrospect, I was (as usual) a few years too early.

I had a story I was in love with and wanted to tell it. I still love that story…Some of my initial readers must love it too, because I'm still asked about it.

But something just didn't work. No one could tell me what it was. I got a lot of "this is a really interesting premise and good story, but it's just not grabbing me." I rewrote almost from scratch three times on top of major reworks and revisions. I tweaked. I nudged. I played with it until I finally had agents interested. I ended up passing on each offer of representation because of other reasons.

In the meantime, while I was working on the fantasy, I jokingly wrote a short story about a YA writer having to write her character's first kiss. I wrote it over several weeks, a scene a week, for a site I had up with my friend Alexia Reed. It was a serial before they were hot (again, timing).

In retrospect, I realize one of the issues with the fantasy was that I was actually hyperaware of Voice and shaping. Yes, shaping it, not finding it. I had a sound and a feel I wanted to give the story through Voice. And while incredibly talented authors who have a strong grasp of their voices might be able to play that way…I was not that girl yet.

Voice felt like such a key element of the story (with two very different worlds colliding and the voice for each character from each land feeling so different) that I struggle with the idea of going back to it. Because gutting my first love sounds like so much fun.

The serial, on the other hand, was this fun, quirky, fast-paced, romp of a Rom Com.

Contrary to popular belief, the main character isn't me. Not all klutzy characters are based on me (well, mostly). When Jeannie read it…Well, here's Jeannie's take:

JEANNIE

I finished reading *It's in His Kiss* and immediately dashed off an excited e-mail to Bria about how much I loved it. She had done something that's very difficult to do: write a story that appears light and breezy and fun on the surface while layering in substance. I told her to extend it into a full-length novel and to start going after contemporary romance author Kristan Higgins's readership.

BRIA

I took her advice and gave the fantasy a bit of a break, focusing on my two loves: YA that dealt with deeper issues and Rom Coms. And that's what brought me my first agent, which was almost immediately followed by an RWA Golden Heart final.

FINDING YOUR VOICE

So you're probably thinking, That's interesting, Owls, but how do I find my voice?

Darned if we know.

Just kidding.

There's a lot to consider as you get started. For some people, their writing voice will sound a lot like their speaking voice. For others, it will be almost unrecognizable to how they speak as a person.

BRIA

My writing voice and speaking voice aren't dissimilar. But when people pointed it out, I realized something a bit unsettling: my speaking voice became more like my writing voice the clearer my writing voice grew.

It was as if I found my true voice and then it grew past the page.

This won't be true for all authors, especially in regard to the genre they write. Can you imagine if I wrote 1950s Noir, *Eh, doll face?*

Your Core Voice is probably not going to come in your first draft or second. You might not even find it in your third.

As a matter of fact, in an Owl Books Poll, over half of writers stated it took reworking more than one manuscript multiple times to feel like they had a grasp of their voices and how to use them.

Both of us reworked and rewrote our first book multiple times. We learned a lot that way. Some of the best growth we experienced was directly from taking feedback from those first books. As we began working together, the feedback on the first three to five pages typically out-numbered the actual words written. There were questions and concerns and challenges and praise.

Once, someone was looking over my shoulder as I started my read-through of one of Jeannie's first chapters and the person told me she would literally cry if she opened a document with that much ink on it.

I'm the opposite in regard to feedback. Once, Jeannie sent me back a critiqued manuscript. I opened it and was annoyed to find she'd sent me the wrong document. I emailed her to let her know she'd sent me almost no notes in this version and I'd wait to get her updates before I dove in.

Come to find out, she'd sent me the right document. We'd reached our next plateau. The things we had been working on were now part of our writing work, not our revising time. This isn't to say we'd perfected those things. Everything is a pattern of growth and plateau, and then more growth.

This was the second time I realized the game had completely changed. Our feedback became different—just as heavy, but different. We'd both found our voices and after another manuscript had learned to harness them most of the time...and so the level of feedback changed with the level of work we were doing.

I wish I could say things got easier, but they didn't. They got harder—in the best possible way.

LETTING GO OF YOUR INTERNAL EDITOR

What is your internal editor? It's that nagging whisper in our heads that persistently tells us there's something wrong with what we've just written and we need to fix it immediately.

When you're putting words on the page for the first time, your sentences will inevitably come out rough. They won't say exactly what you meant to say. You might get frustrated. You might get so frustrated that you must go back and fix that chapter or that last page or even that last line until you're absolutely happy. Your internal editor won't let you move on until the line is perfect.

It's okay to be a perfectionist. It's okay if your writing process requires that you polish one chapter before moving on to the next. Who are we Owls to judge? We all have our own processes.

But for the purpose of discovering your Core Voice, we highly suggest you turn off the editor and give yourself permission to try new things. You don't have to show anyone. It'll be our little secret.

The only way to find your voice is to write and write and write. You want to build your confidence and your level of comfort, and the best way to do that is to experiment and explore rather than concentrate so hard on getting every word right—because you don't know what right is yet.

Now that we've identified our basic building blocks for the Emerging Voice, let's delve into how growing past those can help you shape your Core Voice.

If you're not knowledgeable about literary devices, you need to be. Below are some of our favorites with explanations about how they can help you draw out and enhance your Voice.

While these are our favorites, we recommend grabbing a list of common devices and keeping it next to you as you read your favorite authors. Watch for what techniques work for you as a reader and what doesn't. What can you steal, make your own, and bend to your voice? What's a good tool to keep packed away just in case?

Start thinking about those tools, as we look at some common examples of English literary devices.

WORD CHOICE

The job of word choice is to go beyond just informing the reader what an element is. Word choice tells us more about setting, character, and motivation than actions often do. We Owls think differently about word choice and how we each use it, so let's break it down.

BRIA

Most of my word choices don't happen in the Disaster Draft. I often type words in ALL CAPS if I'm not sure I'm happy with the choice, and there are a lot of those in the drafting round of writing. As someone who wants to get the story on the page as quickly as possible, slowing my stride hunting for the perfect word right then doesn't work well for me. Sometimes those CAPS stay in place for a round…or two…or three. They stay until I'm happy I've found the right word.

But when I come back around on my first read-through, I know that word choice is vital. This isn't a place to skimp on time and effort. My choices are typically focused on pacing and humor. After that, they do certain things for me.

For example, there's a difference between:

She shoved her hair out of her face and shot a hot look his way, quirking her lips up in what she knew clearly stated, Not in your hottest fantasies, jackass .

AND

She tucked her hair behind her ear and glanced up at him, giving him a grin she hoped said, Not in your wildest dreams, buddy .

The actions are the same, but in each one I'm trying to layer in different things about what the character is thinking. In the first example, my heroine is more confident, maybe even…cocky? The vibe definitely has more of an overtly sexual overtone than the second one.

It would have been easy to write, "She looked at him, thinking he was pushy." But what would that tell us in comparison to the two examples above? The previous statements give us flavor—give us Voice.

My goal for my first real draft is to make these word choices inform character, motivation, and story, not just to act as place settings that relate information.

Each word is a tiny key that opens part of the huge lock that is the story. Think of every section of Voice we're discussing as one number in a pass code. The pass code opens the door to your most powerful writing.

There are no wasted words—no useless moments—in a tight piece of writing. If it isn't doing something (strengthening character, moving the story forward, setting the tone, utilizing the pace, etc.), then why is it there?

The answer should never be only "because the reader needs to know this" or "because I loved it."

If it's the first, then find a way to show them. When it's necessary to divulge information, it should be done seamlessly. If it's the second...ouch. If loving something is the only reason for having it on the page, it's hard to defend. If the passage falls flat, you have this thing sitting in your book making people wonder what you were thinking.

Better to love it on its own in a chopped file.

JEANNIE

I was surprised when I learned how often agents would stop reading a manuscript very early on, citing poor or weak word choice. This made me pay attention to my use of words.

I also don't fret over picking the perfect words in the first draft, or perhaps not even the second or third draft. This is very much a final draft phase for me, when I can look at sentences as a whole and see where there's an imbalance. Then I go along and mark "WC" to tell myself to pause there and think of a word that's stronger, more succinct with high impact, when I come through with revisions.

An unusual word inevitably makes the reader pause a little. I don't want the reader to stumble over words unnecessarily just because I think a word is awfully cool. There has to be a good reason to draw attention to a word choice if it's unusual.

Because I write historicals, setting and time period also play into word choice. Often in the first draft I have words that sound too modern or don't quite fit. They may not evoke setting and time as well as they could.

A STUDY OF WORD CHOICE

An author's use of words is not something you want to stick out at you upon reading. Just like you don't start writing a book saying, I'm going to have a great Voice in this story. You don't read a story ogling the words. At least you shouldn't if the author has done his or her job. It's quite educational to reread a favorite story and actually pay attention to the author's use of words as a tool and not just as communication.

Word choice can be one the most vital decisions an author can make. One of our favorite authors is Laura Florand. She writes love stories that straddle the world between Romance and Lit. Her first stories take place in Paris in the high-end world of chocolatiers and pastry chefs. The romance of France—Paris specifically—and the overtly passionate worlds that evolve in just about every kitchen, let alone the artisan ones, allow her to have such rich, fluid, gorgeous language that word choice is key in her work.

Florand uses words that you simply devour (pun intended), which wouldn't work in other people's writing. Her Signature Voice is so solidly set within her style that it feeds into her setting and story. All of the components of her voice become inseparable from one another—and most of that richness is fed directly by word choice. We'll look more closely at Florand's word choice in the Imagery section.

WORD USAGE IN ACTION
EDGAR ALLEN POE'S *THE TELL-TALE HEART*

We highly recommend studying Edgar Allen Poe, not only because he's a master of his craft, but because many of his memorable works are short stories. Master short storytellers, by design, aim to make a high impact with the minimum words. Every single word must pull its weight.

"The Tell-Tale Heart" depicts the inner monologue of a man spiraling into insanity. Re-reading the story while paying attention to word usage was a real eye-opener. Poe's use of emotionally charged language creates a desperate tone that makes this portrait of obsession so convincing.

> *"TRUE!—nervous—very, very dreadfully nervous I had been and am; but why will you say that I am mad? The disease had sharpened my senses—not destroyed—not dulled them. Above all was the sense of hearing acute. I heard all things in the heaven and in the earth. I heard many things in hell. How, then, am I mad? Hearken! and observe how healthily—how calmly I can tell you the whole story."*

What are the power words in this opening? The words that evoke emotion and a gut reaction from the reader?

Nervous. Mad. Disease. Hell.

The passage emphasizes those words to give them more weight. Not merely nervous, but "dreadfully nervous." Madness is brought up twice, each time in the form of a challenge as the narrator demands, "why will you say that I am mad?" and "How, then, am I mad?"

There is another idea echoed in the words of the opening paragraph: what are the symptoms of his disease? Sharpened senses. Specifically the sense of "hearing acute," an unusual combination of words that makes the reader pause and take notice. The phrase, "I heard," is then echoed twice.

Poe could certainly have started with the second paragraph in the story where the narrator explains the object of his obsession—the old man next door and his disturbing blue eye. That second paragraph certainly shows us that the narrator is mad. But the first paragraph lays the foundation for the rest of the story on a visceral level with strong words that hammer out the theme of madness as well as hint at what form the madness will take—the narrator's overly acute hearing. Just as the narrator is fixated on these ideas, Poe's word usage forces them into the reader's consciousness from the very first line to the last and his Voice resonates with you long after the story is finished.

BRAIN FLEX

Pick an important passage from your work in progress.

First, why is it important? If you don't know what you're trying to stress to your reader, word choice isn't going to matter.

Once you know that, pick one to three words. No more. Change them to create the effect you're going for.

Remember, too many unusual words can be distracting instead of strengthening. When you're done, read your work out loud and see how the new words sound in their new home.

CHECK IN

Did you power up? Maybe you slowed down the pace to pull attention to something? Did you create a memorable visual?

Knowing what you want to accomplish with word choice can give you the clarity to really use this exercise for an undeniable impact.

STRENGTHENING WORD CHOICE

As you just saw, word choice can bring power to the page. Even the smallest changes create a richer read. With that in mind, there are a few simple practices we've used to improve our own word usage.

Jeannie's a bit of a word nerd who likes to have a lot of words at her disposal, words full of texture and connotation that she can whip out when needed. When she first started writing, she actually had word lists to choose from if she got stuck.

It was a matter of breaking out of her comfort zone during the revision process. When words are first laid down during the drafting phase, they tend to be very common, with less impact. Using a word list (or sometimes a thesaurus) helped Jeannie by offering choices that weren't what automatically came to mind during the first draft.

Bria goes at this another way: playfully. She utilizes her writing toolbox to twist things around, make old things new, and find a fun, fresh angle to look at the ordinary. Bringing the unexpected to the page in just a word here or there allows her to brighten up an ordinary scene with humor or add weight where there might not have been any before. Shifting a few words around allows that without distracting from the forward pacing of the story.

Both of us use the same approach, experimenting with word choices, to get different ends.

REPETITION

Repetition is the repeated use of words in close conjunction for emphasis.

This is not to be confused with an accidental echo. Echoes can detract from a passage because the author is not intentionally stressing the words that stand out.

Repetition is a simple but effective literary device because you'll see the motivation or theme being pushed to the forefront. It can often be called what the Owls refer to as "silver plattering." There is a time and place for handing the reader your intent in an obvious manner. This is one of the best tools for that.

In Rochester's proposal in Charlotte Brontë's *Jane Eyre*, repetition of the common word "very" creates a sense of doubt and anxiousness:

> *"Again and again, he said, "Are you happy, Jane?" And again and again I answered, "Yes."*

The passage below by Charles Dickens is a well-known example where repeated phrases create a frame and it's the words which are not echoed that stand out:

> *It was the best of times, it was the worst of times, it was the age of wisdom, it was the age of foolishness, it was the epoch of belief, it was the epoch of incredulity, it was the season of Light, it was the season of Darkness, it was the spring of hope, it was the winter of despair,*
>
> *—A Tale of Two Cities by Charles Dickens*

Repetition is a great device for drawing attention to a specific idea by emphasizing key words or setting up patterns and rhythms. It's a good technique with a wide range of uses to experiment with as you develop your voice.

ONOMATOPOEIC WORDS

An onomatopoeic word is one that phonetically imitates, resembles, or suggests the source of the sound it describes. Common examples are boom, zap, ping. The letter combinations evoke the sound, which creates a layer of context within the word itself.

Having a list of onomatopoeic words at hand makes it easy to lend variety to the narrative and allows you to layer in sound without having to explicitly call it out. For example: Someone can "walk" out the door, which describes a neutral action. "Walk" certainly gets the job done. But if he "shuffles" out the door, the "sh" sound evokes the drag of his feet over the floor along with the description of motion.

On the flip side, not all your walks or saids or looks need to be changed to create a bit of flair. There's a time and place for bringing in your tools. Pick your moments.

This is a good tool for enhancing Voice because it is an easy method for replacing common words with ones that are more evocative. These words engage more synapses in your brain because of the combination of meaning and sound. (Can you guess this is the cognitive scientist Jeannie speaking here?) Because of this, they stand out to the reader, making your voice more noticeable.

Where can you use these words in your writing? Anywhere you want to draw attention to movement, sound, or emotion—lots of places.

A character can buzz with nerves. You've sat beside that person, right? I always seem to be the girl seated next to that person on a plane. I can feel their emotions coming off them in an erratic wave of energy that feels like a low buzz fed by anxiety.

COLOR CHART – COLOR DESCRIPTIONS

Colors are another potential place to add a little zip to word usage. Instead of something being plain old red, a splash of vermillion adds a sense of pomp to a scene. A vermillion dress certainly sounds special, exotic, eye-catching. But that doesn't mean you should grab all your colors from the large Crayola box all the time.

Red is familiar, immediate, blunt. Seeing red, going red in the face, a dozen red roses. These phrases garner immediate understanding.

There are times when a red-handled machete is exactly what you need to get the job done.

(And there are times when a cliché is exactly what you need—but that's a discussion for another section. The rule is...Don't rule anything out of your playbook.)

Color is a great way to texturize your work and can easily be used in tune with your voice.

For example, Bria's work is low in description. Her books are more focused on action, dialogue, and internal narrative (what we call smartassity).

When she hits you with description, it's for a reason.

Jeannie's worldbuilding is inspired by Asian cinema, where colors are vibrant. On the page, she uses color to punctuate a description and create a specific focus. In My Fair Concubine, the heroine is a simple tea girl from the dusty provinces who is thrown into the glittering capital city:

> *Even the fruit piled in the stalls sparkled like jewels: rosy peaches and startling pink dragonfruit with green-tipped scales.*
>
> —My Fair Concubine by Jeannie Lin

Jeannie's approach to establishing a strong sense of Voice is to create specific moments with extra punch within the story narration and description. Color is one way to do that, with the goal that a reader experiencing this description has a sense of a unique perspective viewing this scene and a unique voice recreating it. A specific image—a dragonfruit in the marketplace—gives a visual that will grab the reader's attention.

You can see that while "color" seems like a simple topic, the use of it is a powerful tool in your voice toolbox.

If Bria suddenly started using richer, lusher colors in her quick hits, it would clash with her Core Voice. The only way she could get away with that is if she had a character who was specifically involved in a world like fashion, design, or art, who had that language in her own character voice.

BRAIN FLEX

Choose a visual passage from your own work. It may be the first meeting of two characters or establishing the current setting. Add color to one description, or select a place where you've already used color and make it more pronounced. Whatever you choose, make the color usage significant.

CHECK IN

Once done, reread the passage. How does that pop of color make the passage more memorable?

PERSONIFICATION

Personification is attributing human qualities, emotions, or actions to an inanimate object, setting, or occurrence.

At first glance, this may not seem like a device that would enrich your voice, but every tool has its place in the toolbox.

Forces of nature are often personified as we read of the sky weeping and the wind howling. Storms are angry—or so we're told.

By imbuing the surroundings with emotion, the mood of the scene becomes more visceral and intimate. Personification adds connation and layers in additional nuance.

The environment isn't the only thing you can personify. Descriptions such as "an angry rash" or "a lonely island" help us to view the object the way the POV character does.

PORTMANTEAU

Portmanteau used to be a far less common device. It's become a more common way of speaking nowadays.

Portmanteau is combining words together to create a new word. One of the most obvious ones that jumps to mind is Labradoodle. Who would have thought we'd make up a poodle-Labrador mix and just squish the words together?

This device adds flavor to your writing by creating new connotations and twisting words in an interesting way that grabs the reader.

In my YA, *Secret Girlfriend*, my character was talking about her rival, who just happened to be the captain of the cheerleading team. But the character, talking about the rival in a derogatory way, called her a cheerdealer instead. It gives a clear sense of the dislike she feels and the underlying belief that the cheerleader is manipulating the situation in a way that uses her status.

ANACHRONISMS/ANACHRONYM

These are words and phrases that are technically incorrect for the time period of the work. Usually when anachronisms pop up, they're seen as mistakes or oversights by the author, but this device can be used intentionally to establish an author's Core Voice.

An example would be deliberately using modern speech in a historical piece in order to create a story that is more contemporary and accessible. On the flip side, speech that sounds historical can be used in a contemporary story.

For example, the word "rake" is one you see in historical context. But it's also one you'll see contemporary writers use with their romance-reading characters. It says, "Oh, this character is in. She knows what a rake is. She's a romance reader." It adds to the story, enriching it, without a deep explanation.

IMAGERY

Imagery is using descriptive language to create a visual point of reference.

This is probably already in your toolbox—creating pictures and actions with words is second nature to writers. The job now is to have a greater understanding of imagery to draw your reader deeper into the read.

To begin, ask yourself where you can bring in imagery that would tell a truer story than just what the action or descriptions would convey? As Picasso says, "Art is a lie that tells the truth."

In terms of using imagery to enhance and develop your Core Voice, it's a matter of challenging yourself to use more potent imagery that reflects your perspective.

Imagery can be as elaborate as Edgar Allen Poe's description of the plague in "The Masque of the Red Death". Like in the previous Poe example, the visuals in this opening paragraph have lasting implications for the entire story:

> *The "Red Death" had long devastated the country. No pestilence had ever been so fatal, or so hideous. Blood was its Avatar and its seal—the redness and the horror of blood.*

Poe cleverly gives his plague a name that invokes a visual—"Red Death". His voice comes out strongly in the descriptions he uses to support this imagery. Blood is aligned with redness and horror—which is a perspective we are all familiar with. We are naturally disturbed by the sight of blood. But the use of the description "Blood was its Avatar and its seal" transforms the disease into something otherworldly and fatalistic. Blood marks your doom. Imagery is not just for laying out setting, characters, or objects. In fact, imagery can be even more powerful when it is used to illustrate something outside of physical description.

Laura Florand creates a warm and nostalgic mood in the opening of *The Chocolate Rose* as she describes a summer day through the description of an old white-haired couple:

> *A bright feeling seemed to glow...in the old, worn happiness of a white-haired couple walking hand in hand, whose love for each other had been used and worked like fifty-year-old shoes into something so exactly fitted to them that those bright new lovers wouldn't recognize it in their high-heeled love.*

Aside from the white hair, the imagery does not focus on what the couple looks like, but rather their connection to each other, which is described as "used and worked like fifty-year-old shoes into something so exactly fitted to them." The visual is of these perfectly comfortable shoes in contrast to pointy-high heels.

Florand's imagery is deliberately chosen to tap into familiar emotions. Combined with her vivid descriptions, her Signature Voice enhances and deepens the sense of nostalgia and the impact of the scene.

BRAIN FLEX

Part 1: Choose a scene in your work that does not currently have much description. Instead of going through the entire passage and laying down description from start to finish, focus on one specific visual to convey the atmosphere and tone of the scene.

Part 2: Choose a passage where you describe a character's emotional state or a strong reaction to something. Try inserting a strong visual in the scene to highlight and enhance the emotional impact.

SIMILE AND METAPHOR

Many of the examples in the imagery section made use of simile and metaphor.

Simile is when an object, person, place, or idea is compared to something unrelated to make the description more vivid or add context:

> *Alice looked up, and there stood the Queen in front of them, with her arms folded, frowning like a thunderstorm.*
>
> —*Alice's Adventures in Wonderland,* Lewis Carroll

Metaphor is when the comparison is implicit or hidden:

> *All the world's a stage.*
>
> —*As You Like It,* William Shakespeare

Similes and metaphors can be used to expand an idea and increase the impact of a description. By being less direct, the author is able to shift the connotation and strength of the thing being compared. When considering Core Voice, similes and metaphors provide a key opportunity for putting your unique stamp upon your writing. Rather than relying on common or clichéd metaphors, the imagery you choose as well as the language and tone of your similes and metaphors will establish your distinctive Voice.

BRAIN FLEX

Look for one of your similes or metaphors. What does the comparison describe?

Above we referenced Shakespeare's "All the world's a stage" from As You Like It as a famous metaphor. There are several reason this is so apt for the scene:

- Shakespeare is hyperaware of the duality of comparing the world to a stage while creating the world on a stage.
- He has shown that the world is narrower where others might go broad. A stage is only what is in view...In reality, the world is beyond that.

- The character who recites this soliloquy is in a place where his entire being is about acting a part for the world around him, making him the character on the stage.

CHECK IN

Looking at your own passage, how does the simile or metaphor strengthen the view of the character or conflict? If all it's doing is making a comparison, how can you twist and play with it to tell us more about the unspoken truths on your page?

We've talked about what we call "silver plattering." Both of these tools are great work-arounds for giving information without an obvious "As you know, Bob . . ." info-dump situation. You can lay out your story's truths in a more artful and less heavy-handed way.

SENTENCE STRUCTURE

If you recall, when we touched on Emerging Voice we discussed the basics of sentence structure.

Now, as you develop your Core Voice, it's important to dive deeper into sentence structure, which is specifically how your sentences are put together. Are they long, do you tend to use fragments, or maybe you have repetitive noun/verb flow? Each of these is a different way to construct sentences. None of them are wrong, unless you fall into overuse.

When you examine your writing down to the sentence level, you may find some features you weren't aware of. For instance, perhaps your paragraphs sounded all fine in and of themselves, but it turns out each of them starts with the same format of pronoun followed by an action:

He went...

He sat . . .

He lifted his sword...

Sentence structure is one of the major defining characteristics of your voice, and it's invisible—but it's not. If you take a closer look, you can spot it and readers can certainly sense it. Or rather, they'll sense if you have awkward sentence construction. In many ways, the goal of sentence structure is to be unnoticeable.

Sentence structure is one of the most underdeveloped parts of Voice. All authors have patterns they comfortably fall into. However, this can quickly lead to prose that sounds monotonous.

Sentence structure plays into cadence, rhythm, and pacing as well as other elements of Voice. We'll look at more ways to break structure habits in some of the other Voice elements coming up.

BRAIN FLEX

He went to the store. It was late at night. The store was a block away. He walked past the school. At the store he bought eggs. He went home. He baked a cake.

Focus on the sentence structure and content while rewriting this for each of the following situations.

1. A fast-paced adventure
2. A journey of grief
3. A lead-up to a fun date

CHECK IN

How did you vary your sentences to convey the mood and tension? There is no right or wrong approach here. Grief for some may come out as terse, staccato statements. For others, in long, winding reflection. The point is to play around with different combinations and be aware of varying techniques.

CADENCE

DEVELOPING YOUR OWN CADENCE AND RHYTHM

By building on sentence structure, we're starting to move beyond the basics and are on to another essential element of developing your Core Voice: cadence and rhythm. This section dives deeper into the structure of sentences, how they flow together, and the patterns that tend to emerge when you write.

Part of developing your Core Voice is becoming aware of these elements in your reading and writing. The tips in this section describe ways to examine the underlying sentence structure used to create your individual writing cadence and rhythm.

Cadence is one of those things we know when we hear it. It's the pattern you make with your voice and words. Think of a Southern belle and the soft flow of how their speech is typically portrayed. Or the poetic ebb and flow of the Irish cadence.

These two examples show you how a pattern creates a certain cadence and how it can stand out and become recognizable for readers.

Cadence and rhythm are rooted in the underlying sentence structure. They contribute to the flow and tempo of the passage and encompass all the patterns, pauses, and stops that can best be experienced when the words are read out loud.

Have you ever listened to an inexperienced actor or student read poetry or Shakespeare out loud? All you hear is the ABABAB of the structure. A seasoned actor takes the words and layers them on top of the base structure, bringing out the underlying cadence written there in a more meaningful way through added punctuation and timing.

The trick is to find what works and use it for your power moments while not overusing a pattern until it becomes meaningless or distracting.

POETRY AND MUSIC

COLLECTING IMAGERY, PHRASING, AND INSPIRATION

When you think of words flowing, poetry immediately comes to mind. By its very nature, poetry has to create a cadence based on the structure and word choice.

If you feel poetry isn't your thing, it's still an interesting technique to try because you can find many short poems to fit your purpose. Instead of reading a full-length novel or short story, you can finish studying a short poem by setting aside thirty minutes to an hour. The goal is to pay attention to how the poem uses devices such as sentence length, word choice, line breaks, and punctuation to generate its rhythm.

JEANNIE

Since my Tang Dynasty romances take place in China, reading translations of poetry from that era helped me recreate the feel of the time period, as well as develop a sense of drama through cadence. The poems also provide a reference point for period-appropriate imagery. My historical action/adventure romance, *The Sword Dancer*, was inspired by a famous eighth-century poem:

> *When her dance began, her movement was rapid and fierce like furious thunder shaking heaven and earth.*
>
> *When her dance ended, her swords slowed down*
>
> *Invoking thoughts of a mighty river or ocean regaining its shiny reflection.*
>
> —*Observing the Sword Dance of a Disciple of Madame Gongsun*, Du Fu.

This excerpt illustrates the dramatic nature of Chinese poetry and the tendency to use nature metaphors. My narrative voice is both influenced and strengthened by adopting the phrasing and symbolism I find in translated works from the period during which my stories are set—much like an author writing Regency-set fiction might draw influence from Jane Austen.

This practice is not only for historical authors who are trying to recreate historical language. It's a way to look into interesting and creative examples of phrasing and word usage that you may not find in your day-to-day reading.

BRIA

While I don't typically use poetry to get into my creative space, music in many ways does the same thing for me. Not only does the sound evoke the emotions I'm looking to carry through my book, but the cadence of the lyrics often brings about new ways to think about how I structure sentences.

I'd challenge those of you who only listen to the sound of music to listen to the words and note how so many musicians can tell an entire story in three minutes. Yeah, yeah, yeah. I'm going to say it: country music is great for this.

When looking at poetry or music, find the natural emphasis in each stanza. Does it fall on a particular word? How does this impact the way you read it out loud? Finding the anchor point shows you how to read the sentence according to the author's intent.

BRAIN FLEX

Pick a poem and read it while paying attention to the language usage. What word or phrase in the poem stood out the most? Why? If poetry is not your thing, feel free to pick something short. Like a haiku. Do not pick a limerick.

Now choose a song and read over the lyrics. What words or phrases catch your attention? Why?

CHECK IN

Most songs average three to four minutes and tell an entire story. When paying closer attention to the poem or song, did you notice any elements or devices that you hadn't before? Did they make you appreciate the piece in a different way? Store those details in your bag of tricks.

PACING

As we've mentioned previously, pacing at its most basic is how quickly or slowly the story moves. Is it a fast-paced thriller or a slow-building mystery? On one level, pacing also speaks to readability. Are the scenes trudging along because the reader is struggling to get into the story?

When we dig deeper, pacing directly affects the dynamics throughout the story. It's not limited to how quickly a story reads. It's not like running a race and making sure your splits are even. A book rarely keeps the same pacing from start to finish.

There are a couple things that need to be considered about pacing before we even discuss it in terms of Voice.

First, it should not be a static thing.

When you study pacing, it should feel like a living, breathing entity. It is the part of your manuscript that should have the most depth of change from beginning to end.

Pacing isn't a straight line. It should ebb and flow as the story progresses. Think of pacing as the tides of your book. Do you pull people in quickly, and then slow things down? Does the tempo of the read increase with rising tension?

Pacing as it pertains to Voice is important for not only keeping the pages turning, but ensuring the intended turning points, high points, and emotional points have the appropriate oomph. Are you slowing down unintentionally when nothing happens, so it starts to drag? Are you speeding through your emotional hits? There's nothing worse than speeding past something vital to the story and not realizing it because of the author's pacing.

ADDING DYNAMIC PACING TO YOUR SCENE

JEANNIE

When I critique manuscripts from beginning writers, I often suggest adding in highs and lows within a scene. Part of that is plot and tension, but a significant part of it is the flow of the narration. The scene will start with a particular pace and continue from start to finish with no pauses to highlight a shocking surprise or a moment of doubt. Or the pace doesn't speed up to convey a sense of urgency.

When there are no levels to break up the pattern and flow of the sentences, a scene becomes monotonous. Some of this might be due to the external story events—maybe not enough is happening in the scene, there's nothing at stake, or there's no sense of risk—but adding in more action alone will not solve the problem. The points of rising and falling tension within a scene should be supported and enhanced by the underlying sentence structure.

Imagine you are watching a movie, and there's about to be a big reveal. What's inside the bag the character is holding? The camera focuses on the bag, then pans to everyone's faces as they watch with anticipation. Next you see a close-up of the hand opening the bag, followed by a reaction shot.

If the movie scene unfolded in real time it would look something like this: the man reaches for the bag, opens it, and there's a gasp of shock afterward. We know what happened, and we understand that the witnesses are shocked, but we don't feel that build of suspense and anticipation ourselves. The camera work has artificially slowed down time to create a certain effect.

The camera is doing the job in film that your underlying sentences need to do in a written scene. Use your prose to focus in close, to draw out certain moments, and to pan around to take in every character's reaction when appropriate.

The way that an author chooses to execute these important moments—or just the fact that an author has selected certain key moments to highlight—speaks to their Core Voice.

The short story "The Lady or the Tiger" demonstrates this idea of pacing for tension in a few short pages in a way most novels can't manage over several chapters.

At the end, the hero is left to choose between two doors: one with the aforementioned Lady behind it and the other with...Well, I'll let you guess.

The hero is given a clue by the heroine, but is she trustworthy? Even he doesn't know.

The author, Frank R. Stockton, stops here to give us details that build the suspense and terror for the hero and the anticipation of how everything could go wrong in the blink of an eye. The onlookers in the scene cheer—all eyes are on him. He, the only person not watching the door, is watching his heroine, wondering if she will betray or save him.

So, which is it?

The reader needs to follow the pace of the story for the clues that lead to that moment. The entire story is based on building up the suspense surrounding one single climactic decision. Given that the decision is not explicitly revealed, the anticipation itself becomes the end goal rather than a device to support the reveal. It's a great example of using pacing for impact.

CREATING PAUSES

One of the ways pacing can be controlled is through manufactured pauses.

In music, it's important to "play the pauses," as they say. The rests and stops are as important as the notes—perhaps even more so. A dramatic piece of music with a sudden stop makes your ears perk up.

In writing, these rests and rhythms are created by punctuation and line breaks and sentence fragments.

Here is a stripped down example from the final scene of *The Heart of Darkness* by Joseph Conrad:

> *"His last word—to live with," she insisted. "Don't you understand I loved him!"*
>
> *"The last word he pronounced was—your name."*

The em-dashes create pauses in dialogue, which is one step toward establishing the tone of the conversation. Now look below at what happens when we add in the exposition interspersed with dialogue. Here is the more fleshed-out exchange:

> *"His last word—to live with," she insisted. "Don't you understand I loved him!"*
>
> *I pulled myself together and spoke slowly. "The last word he pronounced was—your name."*

In the excerpt, the content itself is emotionally charged and the narrator's actions—

pulling himself together and speaking slowly—illustrate his hesitation. This is a place where the author deliberately inserted a drawn-out, uncomfortable silence. The reader also experiences this pause and anticipates what will come next.

Here's the actual excerpt from the published version:

> *"His last word—to live with," she insisted. "Don't you understand I loved him—I loved him—I loved him!"*
>
> *I pulled myself together and spoke slowly.*
>
> *"The last word he pronounced was—your name."*

The fiancée's repeated entreaty emphasizes her desperation and also has the effect of adding additional words. As a result, her plea is lengthened and the narrator's silence becomes more pronounced. Also, the narrator's action as he hesitates is broken out onto its own line. The additional line break draws out the uncomfortable pause further.

Notice how little changes like supporting tags, additional line breaks, and minor description can do a lot to alter the pacing of a passage.

Notice how the little changes like supporting tags, additional line breaks, and minimal description can do a lot to alter the pacing of a passage.

JEANNIE

When giving feedback, I often make a suggestion for a change, and then qualify that it should be done with only one or two additional lines. Often when a section needs something more, that "something more" is not a whole new scene or paragraph. That would significantly alter the pace, and probably in a negative way that goes against the intent of the writer. What I'm looking for is just a dash of salt to make the moment stand out. Keep this in mind as we go into the exercise.

BRAIN FLEX

Choose an emotional highpoint in your manuscript. It doesn't have to be the book's climax, but it should be a place where you want readers to take an emotional hit or pause. Read through it once and begin by highlighting the emotional impact point.

Look at the surrounding sentences for the build and falling action on either side of the impact point.

Do each of those slopes adequately lead up to and away from the significant moment at the right pace to heighten the emotional effect?

Brainstorm ways you can enhance the payoff. Which pacing tools mentioned in the above section could speed or slow the progression as needed?

CHECK IN

Remember, this is about little Voice tweaks, not adding a significant amount of content, backstory, or plot. When it comes to emotion, you're usually looking to only add or take away a little at a time to achieve your goal.

PART V

BEYOND THE BUILDING BLOCKS

SOLIDIFYING YOUR CORE VOICE

Now that we've looked at the foundation of your Emerging Voice and how to broaden those basics to move up the slope to Core Voice, let's talk about what solidifying your Core Voice looks like.

The basics are important because without them, there's no growth. But how do we move beyond that? There are many approaches we can expand on using those basic building blocks. Get ready for strategies and techniques that will make even the strongest voices stronger.

LOOKING OUTWARD

Up until this point, we've done a lot of looking at what you have on the page right now. Writers shouldn't forget that they're readers and they need to fill their creative wells. Sometimes the best way to develop beyond your current skill set is to study the works of those who have gone before you.

READING OUTSIDE YOUR GENRE

Every genre has its clichés. We don't mean clichés like "dark as night." We mean clichés like "The Butler Did It." Unless you're writing a romance and the butler turns out to be a hot hero who gets the countess, you're probably going to want to rethink that.

It's easy to fall into clichés, to miss them, to accept them as canon instead of tired storylines. We want more than that for you.

Reading outside your genre shows you a fresh way to attack all things story and Voice.

BRIA

Let's go back to my very first romance read, *Romancing Mr. Bridgerton*, by Julia Quinn. Until then I hadn't read a contemporarily written romance. My basis of opinion was from studying British Literature and the stereotypes of modern romances as an undergrad. Quinn's books made yet another shift in how I thought about romances. Even how I read the originals. Austen, for example is both lighter and deeper than our first reads allow us to believe.

Quinn's work showed me some of the ways the writers of Austen's time meant their work to be read by their contemporaries, which was an ah-ha moment for an English major like me!

This first realization occurred to me in a scene where the heroine does something that the hero feels was crossing the line. He's mad. He's upset. He's rethinking how he's always viewed her. But he doesn't yell. And the heroine thinks, Oh, he'd only yell and get really angry if he actually cared about me. That's the type of guy he is. With everyone else, he just lets those things fly by him.

Toward the end of the book, the heroine does something else (she was much more adventurous than we were led to believe!), and the hero feels she's putting herself in danger...and flips the heck out. Yelling, pacing, forcing her into a carriage to get her away from possible discovery.

At no point does the author say, "LOOK! Look what I did there! Two hundred pages ago I mentioned he only gets upset if he cares, and now he's upset. Aren't I clever?" She actually doesn't even have the heroine realize it. She has used the act of trusting her reader to remember that part from the beginning of the book to make the end of the book richer. And she uses this device to show us the growth of the romance arc.

This was not my view of romance before I started reading the genre, and it began the deeper challenging of my views on all genres, causing me to reread some of my favorites and pick up more new-to-me authors and genres. Some of my deepest learnings as a writer have been as a reader.

JEANNIE

After finishing a manuscript, I give myself permission to go on writing strike. I refuse to write or revise for two weeks. Refuse! Even if there's another deadline looming! (Bria insists this is too brief to actually call it a writing strike. She says it's just a break between projects, but I'm calling it a strike, dagnabbit!)

During my strike, I catch up on my to-be-read pile. I take this as an opportunity to clean my palate and read outside of my genre. Even though these are meant to be pleasure reads, writer Jeannie is always studying.

One of the reads that made an impression on me was *The Book Thief* by Markus Zusak. It broke many of the rules of the genres I wrote in. It was told with jumps in time as well as an omniscient point of view. As a result, there was a certain distance from the characters and the protagonist. We get told what their emotions are by an outside observer. The narrator, who is the personification of Death, also tells us what's going to happen in the future. Repeatedly.

So in effect, you know what's going to happen for a lot of the book.

I was intrigued that I was still intrigued! When the book builds toward its climax, I was completely swept up. Despite the emotional distance from the characters. Despite knowing so much information up front. One might think this would lessen the tension, but it actually increased it. Not being allowed deep into the characters' heads made me more invested in them, not less.

The Book Thief was such an outlier in terms of storytelling for me that it made me think and look at the conventions of my chosen genre in a different way.

COPY THE GREATS...LITERALLY

In that vein, why not pick up a few of those great authors now?

BRIA

This sounds like silly advice. I admit, it sounded silly when I heard it as well. But my senior year writing professor made us pick one paragraph at minimum every week and write it out several times. He suggested writing it out five times the first night, and once each night for the remainder of the week.

Did I get anything besides a cramped hand from this exercise?

A surprising amount actually. This was the first time I really began to notice the flow, cadence, rhythm, and structure specific to some of my favorite authors. After a few weeks, what the professor wanted us to see through exercise, we began to see through study. Glancing at a page and assessing style and voice became habit instead of a task.

Writing the words out meant we couldn't speed past them, skim over them, dwell longer in only certain areas that immediately caught our attention. We were just copying...at first. Each word got the same amount of attention because we had to both read and write it.

It didn't take long until copying became a near-memorized transcription. And memory became ingrained. And then the act of rewriting became active evaluation. The muscle-memory, or in this case the memory-muscle, began to show us all those aspects of Voice we had such trouble pinning down before.

It was an eye-opening experiment I highly recommend.

Most writers who have written for a little while will naturally adopt a certain style and tone. That's their beginning platform, their Emerging Voice. Though readers may agree that it's a good fit for the genre and it's readable, they may not find it very memorable. As we just discussed, writers also tend to be influenced by what they read. At some point, a writer's voice may sound like an imitation of someone else's instead of developing into their own unique sound.

For example, Ray Bradbury's writing is expressive and emotional, lacking the metallic, technical feel often associated with science fiction. His perspective tends toward a sense of nostalgia even when describing futuristic events and phenomena.

All of this describes Bradbury's tone and style of writing. To truly examine his voice, the only way is to actually consider the words on the page:

> *It might have been millions of years he'd spent sitting here in the massive glass pendulum watching the world tip one way and another, up and down, dizzily before his eyes until they ached. Since first they had locked him in the pendulum's round glass head and set (it) swinging it had never stopped or changed. Continuous, monotonous movements over and above the ground. So huge was this pendulum that it shadowed one hundred feet or more with every majestic sweep of its gleaming shape, dangling from the metal intestines of the shining machine overhead.*
>
> ☐ *The Pendulum, Ray Bradbury*

From the excerpt we can see what makes Ray Bradbury's voice distinctive is a combination of how he lays down words and how he echoes specific concepts and phrases. In this passage he gives us a sense of movement by describing the up and down movement of the pendulum as well as the narrator's dizziness in one breath. Bradbury utilizes complex, run-on sentences, comprised of many short phrases chained together to create a rhythm.

Your voice deserves no less explanation. It will not suffice to think of your voice as a "quirky" or "suspenseful" voice and leave it at that.

The reason Core Voice is complex and hard to describe in a few words is because it is a sum total of style, tone, word choice, sentence structure, cadence, and craftiness that makes your writing uniquely you. It's about all the decisions you make down to the line level. Down to the word.

READING OUT LOUD
NO, NOT YOUR STUFF

We're often told to read our own stuff out loud, but how about other authors?

Grab a book you love and read it aloud. Read it at the pace that feels right. Read it with the tone and vivacity and attitude the words and story lend it to. Read it with swagger. Kill that piece. Fall into it and feel it for the performance it plays out in your mind's eye.

Then, read it again.

And again.

Read it until it feels natural. Until you don't feel like your twelve-year-old self hiding in your room singing into a brush.

Now ask, what changed from that first read? What moved from rote to intrinsically part of the piece as you learned it? What grew and showed itself?

That's its voice.

Those things that pushed your recitation from just saying the words to expressing them with emphasis and feeling. The change came from reading through the voice cues given to you by the author.

Voice cues are a powerful way to know if your voice is coming through.

READING OUT LOUD
NOW YOUR STUFF
BRIA

One of the scariest things I did when I first started writing was a reading marathon with one of my CPs.

She came to my house for ten days. The first five, I read her book to her out loud while she sat with her own copy of the manuscript open making notes and changes, asking me why I was reading something a certain way, marking where I stumbled or had to reread something, hearing the way dialogue was spoken aloud, watching how long it took me to "get" a character and begin to read for her.

Then we switched and she read my manuscript to me.

And wow was it eye-opening...and a wee bit painful.

I could hear what parts sounded immature and amateurish. I could hear all those things I noted above that I made notes and changes as she went.

At one point, my character began her first line of dialogue and I had to stop my CP and ask, What are you doing? since her voice had shifted to this upbeat, clippy thing. She answered, "I'm doing you doing your character."

On the upside, I obviously had dialogue voice down!

Which brings us to a difficult question to hit head on: Does your voice match your story?

Notice we didn't say your genre.

For example, many successful, prominent authors have more modern voices while writing historicals. For some this works incredibly well. It's their Signature Voice and they make it work in their genre. Instead of trying to shoehorn their voice into a box that isn't theirs. They use their voice and shape it into something that will.

Another great example is *The Martian*, Andy Weir. The protagonist manages to give us a ton of scientific details showing how he stays alive while being a completely dismissive smartass. The tone and word choices don't exactly say genius. But, when you know the character's background is being the flight expert in both mechanical engineering and botany, as well as the fact that he's been chosen to be one of six on a mission to Mars...well, obviously he's tweaking the "stuffy scientist" mold with his voice. The voice is what pulls you along, doesn't let you go, and feeds you a bunch of data that would bore you in a classroom setting.

If you're unable to shape your Core Voice into your current genre in a saleable way OR you're unhappy with the result, the question becomes... change your voice or change your story...or something else?

Each author needs to answer that for themselves. It's a far more complicated question than it first appears.

Story is what brings us to our work. Most authors start because they have a story to tell. I've never heard someone say, "You know what? I'm really excited about my voice. I think I'll write a book."

Sorry, Voice. Never heard that.

For some, small tweaks will fine tune one or both and bring them into alignment. For others, a complete examination of why it's not working and if you might be more successful if one is adjusted. Then there are those talented (or lucky) few who for some, the juxtaposition is part of what will, perhaps with some effort, make their writing work.

How do you know if this is you?

Most people aren't going to sit down, start typing, and write in a beautiful, clear, voice their own instinctually.

MATCHING THE STORY

Earlier, Bria talked about not finding her voice until she tried a new genre. When we talked to a group of authors about this, many of them stated that they'd always felt like it was "almost there" until they tried changing genre or point of view (POV), which is who we are viewing the story through.

The most common ways to tell a story are first and third person.*

First person POV would be someone telling you the story directly: I did XYZ.

First person past tense POV means they already did it: I walked down the street.

First person present tense POV means they're doing it now: I'm walking down the street. In first person, you know exactly what the person whose head you're in knows. It's like listening to their thoughts from inside their head. You hear their inner dialogue and ideas. The flip side of that is if the narrating character doesn't know something...neither does the reader.

Third person past tense POV is as if the story is being told about the person in the past: He walked down the street. Or, they walked down the street.

Third person present POV (very uncommon) would be: He walks down the street, looking at the leaves.

There's a little more playing room with third person for presenting the reader with the character's knowledge. You will more likely be telling the story from multiple characters' vantage points, giving the reader more detail. Depending on which POV you pick for a scene, the reader will be impacted differently and get different information.

And finally, and currently more uncommon than twenty years ago, third person omniscient.

This is told in the same style of he/they/etc., but with the added twist that you're seeing the story from what used to be called "God's Eye"–otherwise known as "the reader knows all."

This has currently fallen out of fashion in most genres, but we've seen several great books highlighting it again recently, such as The Book Thief, mentioned earlier.

You can see that deciding how to tell your story can be an incredibly powerful tool. A shift in POV can create a different dynamic in an author's work and move their writing forward.

*For a more detailed breakdown of point of view, see Appendix A in the back of this book.

LOOKING INWARD

In the previous section, we considered the broader questions of genre and audience. Now it's time to dive back into your manuscript.

In the previous section, we considered the broader questions of genre and audience. Now it's time to dive back into your manuscript.

AMPLIFICATION

For most writers, elements of your voice are already present when you begin climbing the slope to Core Voice. But that doesn't mean they're strong enough to be noticeable...yet.

To get there, you need to enhance your voice's defining features—project your voice as if you're singing to the back of the room. In the same vein, taking out extraneous words and details can make your Core Voice speak louder. There's less noise and fluff around to distract from it.

JEANNIE

Readers often attribute lyrical passages and beautiful descriptions to my writing, but the truth is most of my sentences are pretty spare. I want to choose my moments so those little accents stand out more. The descriptiveness has become a signature feature that readers remember, but under scrutiny, I actually have minimal description except during key moments in the story. Description is one of the areas I need to improve on, and I get frequent comments that I need to add more.

> *Today she wore a pale green robe, the color almost nonexistent and only there to keep the dress from being white. She tried so hard to be nondescript, to disappear, but her face was likely to be the most memorable one in the quarter.*
>
> *The birthmark over her left cheek was a swirl of dark red. It ran down her face and along the line of her jaw,*

> *stopping just short of her chin. Her complexion was otherwise fair, highlighting the stain even more. It was as if an artist painting her had started to form the shape of her mouth when he'd inadvertently splashed red ink over the paper. He then left it there, finding the stain created a spark of drama beyond mere prettiness. Like finding a blood red peony among the snow.*
>
> —*The Lotus Palace*, Jeannie Lin

This is probably the most descriptive passage in the whole book. It's the impression of the heroine through the hero's eyes. The first expanded description of her the reader sees. But I didn't focus much on her overall appearance. I mention her dress, mostly to say that there wasn't much to it. The rest of the detail concentrates on the birthmark on her face where I devote an obsessive six sentences to a red stain. At the end of it, you don't even know if the hero thinks she's pretty or not or what her eyes or lips look like.

My intention was to amplify the effect of the red birthmark rather than the heroine's overall appearance, or her character as a whole, at that point. I further amplified this by minimizing the remaining description in the rest of this chapter.

What this also allowed me to do was have a book that's considered rich with description, without having general description blanketing every page. I used specific details at targeted locations as a punch point.

My writing has become less flowery with purple prose (though I still veer toward the melodramatic, as you can see). This may be a function of my personal tastes and style changing, or just a little more confidence that the small bits of flair are enough to get the job done without having to whip out so many extra embellishments.

This was just one example of amplification.

Amplification doesn't have to happen through setting or physical description. It can occur in dialogue. It can be the way action scenes unfold. The idea is to choose a moment, a moment you consider important, and make sure the elements of your Voice shine through so it gets noticed.

LAZY DESCRIPTION

Building from the idea of adding specificity and amplification, we can address an issue that lies behind flat writing in a manuscript: lazy description. This is one reason why a scene doesn't come alive for the reader.

Often writers fall back on describing their story world and characters through everyday terms and shortcuts. We assume readers have the same understanding we do, and that they will "fill in the blanks" for us. This doesn't bring any extra richness or insight to the story.

Description isn't just about the visuals. It's about building the story through the readers' internal senses.

JEANNIE

As someone who loves adjectives, it's hard for me to say this, but adjectives are lazy. Or, rather, the over-reliance on adjectives is lazy. And if those adjectives are common and generic, then they're even lazier. My challenge was with character descriptions. Because I could see them clearly in my own head, I'd fail to flesh them out on the page. My heroes tend to be "tall with a dark look about him." How many heroes does that describe?

Authors, particularly those writing within a genre's norms, can rely on certain shortcuts. An easy example of this is the "wallpaper historical" where the author is relying on common reader knowledge of popular Regency historicals to fill in the blanks. This is not necessarily bad. Description isn't the end goal of our books. Without needing to lay out the details, the author instead can focus on character interaction within a very well-known, nondescript stage setting. It's a valid and effective approach, but we should also recognize it for what it is: Lazy description.

In order to combat lazy description, I look for places where my description assumes the reader will just fill in the details. A passage may rely on a few common adjectives to lay out the scene. In those spots, I push myself to be not only more vivid and visual but more creative in the description.

Example from Jeannie's "The Warlord and the Nightingale", a short story:

First attempt:

> *"Hanzo passed through an archway that led into a garden."*

Alternative version #1:

> *"Hanzo passed through an archway that led into a well-manicured garden with bonsai trees."*

Alternative version #2:

> *"Hanzo passed through an archway that led into a garden where the trees twisted low to the ground."*

The first description is passable, but it can be any garden. The second description attempts to specify a well-kept Japanese garden with little bonsai trees—but it doesn't necessarily create a specific visual. The final version is what ended up in the published story.

The third one doesn't just give you a richer visual; it's more immersive. It puts you more presently there. There's also an emotional connotation.

The purpose of the revision was to take a flat, generic description and create a visual using language unique to my voice. Specificity and strong word choice lend authenticity and help build a stronger sense of Voice.

BRAIN FLEX

Choose a descriptive passage in your manuscript. Highlight all of the adjectives.

Are they commonly used or more specific adjectives? Are the common adjectives doing any work or can they be removed?

When you look at them one by one, are they doing the job you want them to?

If not, is it because they're too common, too "busy," or unnecessary?

Adjust accordingly, and then look at the passage as a whole again. Re-highlight and inspect. Make sure you're not overrunning your new work with new problems.

CHECK IN

What you should have seen is a shift to stronger description. Remember this isn't always about adding more flowery prose. Sometimes the simpler word is more powerful. Like we discussed a few chapters ago, the more direct description can sometimes be the more appropriate. There's a place for "red" and a place for "vermillion." It's your job to define those places.

MAINTAINING INTERNAL TENSION

The cardinal rule for all writing is don't bore the reader.

We don't want to have passages the reader can skim. But sometimes we just need to get from point A to point B and the narration reflects that. This can be a description of time passing, or literally someone traveling from one place to another.

Every story has connective tissue. Upon rereading, you may find spots where the narration, for lack of a better word, feels boring. But you need it to move the story forward, so you just can't skip to the good stuff. You may find this issue particularly rampant during that section we dub "The Sagging Middle." The plot drags. The writing drags.

What does this have to do with Voice? A strong Core Voice keeps the reader engaged. It also needs to stay alive even when there's nothing big happening on the page. Your voice needs to stay alive especially when there's nothing big happening. Your voice needs to stay present and active through transitions and slow-paced sections, so that there are no dead parts. Dead spots are missing those elements that make your voice stand out. There's nothing there to wake the reader up or give them a reason to pay attention. For some reason, these spots in your manuscript have been neglected. The fix is to go through in revisions and give them some attention.

Points of tension tend to have many of the techniques we've described: stronger word choice, unexpected sentence breaks, humor, etc.

Note: We are not referring to large chunks of your manuscript that require revision. If you are looking at entire chapters that drag and are considering altering plot or story structure, then the section is not yet ready to be edited for Voice.

Revisions should be the phase in which you strengthen your voice, not edit it out. Authors often speak about revising and polishing a manuscript as if they are one and the same. When editing for Voice, you must make an active effort to identify places where the voice can be enhanced, not just cleaned up.

To liven up these sagging parts, we'll be building upon techniques discussed in prior sections.

GENERAL STRATEGY

1. IDENTIFY DEAD SPOTS.

Distance is key for this. After you finish a chapter or chapters, give yourself time away from the manuscript. When you come back to it with fresh eyes, mark any spots where you feel the narrative is not engaging. If you're still too close to the work (as we often are), enlist a reader to go over the manuscript and ask them to specifically mark places where they felt taken out of the story or disengaged.

2. CAN THE PROBLEM AREA BE DELETED?

Sometimes the best editing tool is the backspace key. It may hurt to cut words, but parts that drag are often repetitive or otherwise unnecessary. Don't be afraid to delete a phrase or line or whole paragraphs that aren't working. As we covered in the amplification section, removing the dead weight can make the writing that remains shine more brightly.

3. THE LINES CONVEY NECESSARY INFORMATION, BUT NEED SOME WORK.

- Can you assert your character's POV more fully?
- Do you need to remind readers of current stakes?
- Does the writing itself need to be woken up?

Notice that making the prose snappier should be the last of your considerations. Flashy writing alone won't save a flat page. Most importantly, you can't cover up a lack of storytelling with clever words. Readers can tell!

Asserting your character's POV is the first strategy listed because if your protagonist has dropped away, then the Voice in the section drops away. The narration becomes detached from the character's sense of tension and anticipation. If the narrator is not engaged, then the reader won't be engaged either. Try inserting a question or observation from the character's mindset. When doing so, you're injecting specificity.

Reminding the reader of the story's current stakes flows from the first strategy. In order to keep the tension alive, sometimes a reminder of why the story is going there will help keep the reader engaged. What sort of concerns does the character have? What are the challenges she is facing? How can the narration convey your main character's hopes and fears to the reader to create a sense of anticipation?

Finally, you can sprinkle in small accents to make the reader perk up and take notice. This is where all your work with word usage, sentence structure, and pacing comes into play. Pick your moments! Center your work around points that you wish to emphasize to the reader.

JEANNIE

Part of my process for finding my voice was trying to figure out why agents and editors "just weren't connecting" with my writing. I took a book I loved, sat down with a highlighter, and started highlighting sentences that were emotionally charged and rife with tension. I was surprised at how often I was marking the page, even in scenes and descriptive paragraphs I didn't initially think of as emotional.

So how do you amp up your voice and take it from "solid" and "well-written" to something that makes people sit up and pay attention?

The highlighting exercise taught me how often successful writers were hitting emotional notes. I went through my capable but unremarkable prose and found lines that were just...blah. Places where the narration was flat and didn't serve the story well. Whenever I found these spots, I wrote the tag "d/b," for "do better." It was a note that reminded me that this passage is lazy. Try a little harder. Give people a reason to listen.

With one line here, a little tweak there, my voice began to emerge from what used to be the dead spots in my writing. I noted some of my general problem areas earlier in this section regarding internal tension. You may find these helpful as a starting point, but as you look in detail at your writing, you'll see where your problem areas and dead spots tend to be so you can target them accordingly.

This strategy was the very last improvement I made before my writing started getting noticed. The changes themselves were minor, but they made the difference between "almost there" and getting called back.

By consistently trying to "do better," you'll get better. That's pretty awesome.

Make it a practice to look over your writing with a critical eye. Your voice will inevitably strengthen as you put in the work to revise.

BRAIN FLEX

Select two unedited pages from your manuscript. Read over the pages and mark up potential points for improvement. Don't pause to fix each concern. Review the entire sample and make notations where changes will need to be made.

Once you are done marking up the pages, go back through and use the strategies listed in this section to enhance the pages. When done, reread the pages to yourself.

Did you do any cutting? How much text did you add to the prior draft? Do you hear your voice coming through more clearly? These are "final edit" revisions, so we don't expect there to be dramatic overhauls.

CHECK IN

Of the changes you made, what do you feel are the biggest "bang for your buck" modifications? Were there any spots where you felt you were trying too hard to tweak for the sake of the exercise? Have a reader do a final pass to see if anything sticks out as distracting or unnecessary.

BALANCE OF DIALOGUE AND NARRATION

The way a writer combines dialogue and narration is one of the key features of their style. Some authors will have entire pages of dialogue with only a few tags to keep the reader oriented. Others prefer large passages of narration with dialogue only occasionally interspersed within the pages. There are masterful writers on each end of the spectrum, so there is no saying which method is right. What you need to examine is:

- How do you currently combine these two elements?
- Is the combination accomplishing what you need it to do?

Readers tune in to dialogue. It's where the good stuff lies. These lines reveal character and forward plot as well as heighten conflict between characters. Dialogue is where your voice can really shine as your characters engage in witty or tense or intimate exchanges.

The juxtaposition of dialogue with narration affects several key building blocks we have already discussed, including pacing and cadence. When editing for Voice, it's important to consider the content of the dialogue, but also to step back and examine how the dialogue is interspersed through the text.

OVERUSE OF DIALOGUE

Snappy dialogue between characters creates a fast-paced and pleasurable read, but too many extended exchanges with little narration in between will risk losing the reader. We call this effect "talking heads."

The reader loses sense of the surrounding action and setting of the scene, and the characters become disembodied as they bounce back and forth in dialogue.

A tip Julia Quinn teaches in her dialogue workshop is to vary sentence lengths so the rhythm doesn't fall into an expected pattern. This keeps the reader engaged and attentive throughout the entire passage. Just as great oral storytellers know how to raise their voices at dramatic points or use strategically placed pauses to draw the audience in, great writers use sentence length to direct the reader.

LACK OF DIALOGUE

Long stretches of narration and exposition without any break can lose the reader. Find exposition that can be replaced with dialogue. This creates emotional context as your characters interact while also moving the story forward. Dialogue allows you to provide the same information in fewer words and in a more conversational and engaging Voice.

DIALOGUE THAT NEEDS A SUPPORTING TAG OR DESCRIPTION

Dialogue and action tags can be used to add more flavor to your narration as well enhance your characters' voice by providing those necessary breaks in rhythm that make a reader take notice.

"Hungry?" She held up her box to him.

He smiled a little. "I'm always hungry when you're around, Célie."

—*All For You*, Laura Florand

BRAIN FLEX

Take one to three pages from an unrevised manuscript. Highlight only the dialogue.

Read through only the dialogue without the narrative in between. Does the exchange make sense and flow on its own?

Is the dialogue spaced far apart with large blocks of narration in between? Does the narration break up lines that should be spoken close together? Are there points in the dialogue that could use an extra pause to drive the point home? Think of how you time the punch line when telling a joke or pause before revealing important information to make sure your audience is listening.

Find an area with a long paragraph of exposition. Replace it with lines of dialogue. How does this change the pacing of the section?

CHECK IN

Using dialogue is a great way to break up long narrative passages. Make sure the dialogue sounds natural and conversational. Replacing long paragraphs of so-called "info dump" with dialogue by just placing quotes around it won't fool anyone!

Dialogue should feel natural while moving the story forward.

No one wants to be around that guy who talks to hear his own voice.

ACCENTS, DIALECTS AND FOREIGN LANGUAGES

If your story has protagonists who are non–English speaking or have an accent or dialect, their speech becomes intertwined with your writing voice. In addition to your new techniques of establishing Voice, you will want to incorporate elements such as the rhythm of their speech or their use of colloquial words into their dialogue or your narration. This feeds into creating an authentic character voice.

We're going to talk more about balancing many character voices with your author voice in the next section, so we'll only touch on a few points regarding foreign languages and dialects here.

There are different opinions about whether or not an author should try to recreate the phonetic sound of an accent or dialect. As always, there is no hard and fast rule. The degree of language to incorporate is up to the author depending on what she wants to accomplish. But we can share a few tips we've encountered that resonated with us.

But wait! Don't just skip ahead if you only write within English-language settings. This section addresses nuances of character speech and Voice that are important for any language.

Every book brings a reader somewhere they've never been. There are word choices that will establish the characters' setting and background instantly. Knowing how to set up your character as a "city girl" or "Midwest hero" is vital. The English-speaking world—even just the US—is a huge place filled with rich dialects and accents.

The use of foreign languages or dialect is a tricky prospect. It's an art to create the cadence and rhythm of any language. Non-native speakers have to study a language or dialect extensively before truly understanding its makeup. With that in mind, occasional hints to represent the native cadence and rhythm and phrasing may be enough to create the feel of authenticity. The caveat here is that if you take those simplified elements too far, the depiction can veer into sounding like a caricature. Keeping these tips in mind will enrich not only your characters but your voice.

First and foremost, if you wish to re-create an accent or dialect, spend some time becoming familiar with actual speakers. Don't shortcut this step by relying on another author's usage or second-hand depictions such as movies and television. If you are basing your construction on a version that is already watered down, you risk creating something that's reductive and even more of a stereotype. Such is the phenomenon of "Dinna fash yerself, lassie," appearing everywhere in historical romance.

One tip regarding dialects (such as a Scottish brogue) is to drop in the dialect early in the book, but once it's established, reduce the usage so it fades into the background. At that point, the reader has already internalized it and doesn't actually have to stumble over repeated "dinnas" and "kinnas" to know the characters are speaking with a brogue.

Another major consideration regarding language is whether to include foreign words and colloquialisms in dialogue or narration. They can enhance your voice or your characters' voices by lending those elements previously mentioned: specificity, distinctiveness, and emotional connotation. How much to incorporate is up to the author, though it's important to note that each use has the potential to pull readers out of the story.

Readers have varying tolerance levels for words they don't understand, and there's no pleasing everyone, so be aware of the choices you are making. When trying to decide which foreign words or phrases to use, it's important to choose your battles. A few key words here and there can give the flavor of a different language, but too many may start to feel obtrusive (or outright irritating to the reader).

On the other hand, words embody and invoke specific ideas and can be very powerful. There are instances where a foreign phrase embodies a certain concept and provides nuance that a direct translation does not. Omerta—referring to the Mafia code of silence—in the Godfather books by Mario Puzo, is an example. Omerta has a different feeling than just saying, "don't be a snitch." There is a deeper meaning ingrained in that culture. Just the fact that there is a specific word for it indicates that omerta is an important concept.

Similarly, the use of jargon or "inside phrases" brings the reader into a hidden world and makes it feel inclusive. In these cases, the words warrant some explanation. If you're going to use the extra verbiage to explain, make them count and make certain they have the intended purpose of enhancing your voice and drawing the reader in.

When making the choice to use a foreign word or colloquialism, it helps if the word can be figured out in context. In general, keep the reader engrossed in the story. The purpose of using native words is to add color and context and immerse the reader in the character's world. If the language usage is causing a high level of confusion, then the words are no longer serving their intended purpose.

An interesting thing to keep in mind is that a person's first language is the language of their heart. The primary language centers in the brain are wired to the limbic system, the seat of emotion. This is the reason people often default into their native language when swearing in the heat of the moment. As a result, it's more organic in narration to drop into native language or colloquialism to stress a moment that is emotionally charged. Common examples of emotive language are what the character calls his mother, father, or grandparents. Phrases the character grew up with are also very close to the heart.

JEANNIE

Since my books are set in China, technically everything you read is "translated." The characters are actually speaking some dialect of Chinese to each other. I opt for creating a period feel in terms of the narration and dialogue, but I also lean on the side of accessibility. I want the book to be readable.

In terms of Chinese words and phrases, I try to choose them carefully. One example is using the term yuan fen instead of just translating it to "fate." In Chinese culture, the concept of fate is prevalent. It's so prevalent that just the word "fate" falls flat, at least to my ear. Yuan fen means the fate that brings people together. It's a concept that my characters, as Chinese, would have close in their hearts. It's also very pertinent to the idea of romance. In English we might say "star-crossed lovers," whereas in Chinese and Asian culture, it's common to speak of "fate without destiny" when speaking of ill-fated love. Two people have yuan fen and are fated to meet, but they aren't fated to stay together forever, lacking destiny. The phrase has so much nuance and authenticity to it that it pulls a reader deeper into the character's voice.

Another consideration along these lines is modern versus historical speech. There are different schools of thought regarding modern speech in historical fiction. It's a balancing act, but I lean toward what's familiar and natural sounding. Readers are filtering your voice and your character's voice through their minds. Linguistic devices like contractions, idioms, common phrases make the prose flow.

Oftentimes, it's tempting to make historical characters sound stiff, but keep in mind that these characters are in their own world and speaking with their peers. They don't sound stilted to one another.

I've mentioned earlier that I read English translations of Tang Dynasty poems to get a feel for the language. My goal is to re-create the cadence of the period without sounding unnatural and without necessarily incorporating Chinese words.

I've been accused of sounding too modern by having a Tang Dynasty character talk about "falling for" the heroine. I accept and expect such feedback because of the authorial decisions that I made up front. I opted for familiarity versus authenticity. In any case, authenticity is an illusion.

In the end, it's the author's choice how they want to shape their voice using dialect, native language, or colloquialism. My word of advice is this: know what effect you're aiming for and have a plan for how to execute it. And then try as hard as you can to hit your mark.

BRIA

Jeannie's commentary about language brings up another point of how we work together.

One of the things I read for in her work is what we laughingly call Outsider Understanding. As I go through, I mark things I had to figure out, that weren't apparent enough in context; things I may have forgotten the contextual meaning of, because the last time the word was used was too many pages previously; and things I just didn't get or had to guess at.

This allows her to make sure that she's hitting her cultural stride while not alienating too many readers. This is one of the reasons it's good to use several beta readers, including ones who may have intimate knowledge of your setting or subject as well as readers who are new to the material.

Jeannie's Core Voice is powerful in that it works as a bridge between cultures. She manages to tell us stories she feels comfortable basing in worlds that are real, but most of us aren't familiar with. In a less detailed Voice, this wouldn't work.

The danger of not using all your tools in your voice arsenal here is that you'll create a surface level stereotype that will be insulting to readers who live in the culture you're representing. Or you'll go too deep, not trusting your voice to create the cultural bridge for you.

Oddly enough, Jeannie also does Outsider Understanding reading for me as well.

As someone who writes YA, my main focus is my teen audience. A lot of authors write YA for adults, but my books are written about teens for teens.

When you write YA with a strong teen voice, there is always the fear of alienating your adult crossover readers. To check for this, Jeannie comments in her critique where I slip too far into "teendom."

LAYOUT OF ELEMENTS

It may come as a surprise, but the visual aspect of a page impacts how the reader views the work and the author's voice.

One of the tips we've picked up along the way (a tip that seems trivial, but it's really quite a big deal) was the "Between the Lines" section in Noah Lukeman's *The First Five Pages*, which mentions the significance of the overall appearance of a page.

By skimming a manuscript and looking at the way the text appears, whether it be filled with heavy blocks of text or pages and pages of dialogue with exposition, you can get a sense of the writer's style. At a quick glance, you can judge how balanced it is without ever actually reading the words.

When we speak about Voice in terms of the written word, it's a tricky thing. It involves how a reader's inner ear perceives the flow of the words and sentences, and also how the eye experiences the text on the page.

There's a reason readers tend to read dialogue and skim through long passages of exposition. Dialogue is filled with white space. It's easy on the eye. Thick, densely packed paragraphs remind us of reading a textbook or an essay. They look like work.

Pay attention to how the page is broken up and the balance between dialogue and narrative. In addition, use line breaks and punctuation to frame your voice and show it off. Line breaks, invisible as they might be, are effective tools.

BRAIN FLEX

Open your manuscript to any page and look at it without reading it.

Does it look dense? Is there an obvious flow that looks easy and inviting to the reader?

If not, how can you adjust your dialogue, prose, and line breaks to create a more visually appealing read that echoes what your Voice is trying to accomplish?

CHECK IN

Appearance can often be just that. A few visual shifts can create a simplified page structure and subconsciously create a faster, easier read.

CONNOTATION AND HUMOR

As we've discussed, one of your core building blocks is word choice.

Remember when we started with the Emerging Voice style descriptions "I have a lyrical voice" or a "I have a funny voice"? This is the opportunity to dig deeper into that emotional description.

One example of a place you can play with this is humor. It's something that can make or break a joke, move the pace along, or cause an ah-ha moment. Often, the thing that makes something funny is a small difference in words.

This is the power of connotation.

BRIA

I was once involved in a twenty-minute conversation about the difference between panties, undies, and underwear. (Welcome to the life of a Rom Com writer.)

As you read those words, you placed your own connotation on them. You likely pictured a different image in your mind for each one.

And yet they're all technically the same thing. If asked for a definition of each, people would probably end up in slightly different places on the details, but when you look at it, they're all just "undergarments women wear." But each word invokes the visual of a different woman, a different situation. You immediately place your own meaning over any word.

You can see how word choice between those three things would make a difference.

One of the shortcut words for my voice is "quirky." I hear it a lot from my readers.

When I'm shifting my words around, looking for the best choice, I remember my Core Voice—what I'm known and appreciated for. When focusing on my Core Voice, I hone in on which of those three words would make the best, smartest impact for the humor of the moment.

And that's what I do.

EASING READERS INTO YOUR VOICE

You've come a long way since we started. Just like with every other craft topic, the first pages of your book are vital for establishing Voice. Some readers give you a chapter, some five pages, some one page, some only give you a line to hook them...or turn them off.

Speaking as a reader, I've had a few books where one or two lines have not only not grabbed me but turned me off. This may not be a bad thing. I may not be that person's reader.

But what if I were?

The trick to initiating readers into your voice is assuming that every time someone opens one of your books, it's possibly their introduction to your voice. Just like in real life, it's easy to misunderstand someone's intentions if you don't know them well.

A perfect example of this is sarcasm.

Sarcastic voices (either author or protagonist) can be very successful in flavoring a story. The problem is, too often when sarcasm enters the picture right off the bat, readers don't know how to take it.

I can't tell you how many times an author has asked one of us to look at an opening because she was getting feedback that her heroine was "a bitch" (beta and editor words, not ours). Usually, there's one of three things going on:

- The heroine is tough, and her toughness is coming across as unsympathetic without backstory.
- The heroine or the author's voice is sarcastic, and the reader hasn't adjusted to the character's voice yet.
- Okay, the heroine really isn't a nice person. Mission accomplished.

If she's just tough or unsympathetic, it's being commented on because that's not coming across in the way you want her to be shown. This probably has to do with how you've introduced her voice.

Looking at the last two situations, both are at least partially a Voice issue. Let's examine ways to fix this without changing your story or character.

Every book is like a new relationship with someone you just met. Assume the first five pages should be your book on its best behavior. Traits like sarcasm, dark humor, ditzy-but-smart, etc.—all of those easily misunderstood characteristics and voices that need to be introduced—need to wait for a bit before diving into a full-on immersion. The goal isn't to start weak. It's to start strong...but approachable. Ease people into those more extreme voices and characters.

Let's stick with the sarcasm example for a moment. If the character is sarcastic in a funny way (as opposed to a downer-type way) then you want to make sure that the reader understands that.

Don't forget that, unlike your CPs, your reader doesn't know you. They don't hear the underlying author voice naturally and they haven't talked with you for months about this project. You're not sitting next to them reading it in the tone you want them to hear.

Baby-step into your story. Sure, if your first line's hook is important, use it. But if that's where you're introducing an extreme character voice, then make sure the line after it shows that your heroine isn't a heartless harpy...She's just a girl having a bad day and rolling her eyes sarcastically at it.

How long would you hang out with someone you didn't know and couldn't get a feel for if the only trait you saw was perceived as negative? Not long. Life is too short for a bunch of negativity and complaining in your life.

The first few pages should be a hit-and-a-pat. Bam! Sarcasm! Show why it's okay. Bam! Hits you again. Eventually, the softening language at each step can go away and the sarcasm is seen in the right light.

Then you can up your ante on your voice and take the world head-on.

JEANNIE

This is not limited to making sure readers understand your characters. It also applies to stepping into a historical or fantasy world.

In the first couple pages of my novels, I pay special attention to the flow of the writing and try to make it as accessible as possible so readers become accustomed to the tones and style inherent in my historical voice.

BRAIN FLEX

Read your first three lines out loud. Do they flow? Are there any places that might stop the reader? Do they showcase or hint at your voice or are they generic lines that anyone could have written?

Most importantly, do they introduce your Voice and character in an accessible way to readers?

CHECK IN

Still not sure?

Give your first two paragraphs to several people who know nothing about your story. Ask them to describe the main character in three words just from that—did they answer the same way? If so, great!

If not, rinse and repeat.

IDENTIFYING YOUR FATAL FLAWS

We've looked at a lot of different ways to enhance what you already have. But we don't want to ignore the fact that we all have weaknesses too. We call these our Fatal Flaws...waiting to be hunted down and destroyed.

JEANNIE

When it comes to developing your Core Voice, it helps to identify your writer quirks so you can address them. For example, I tend to start sentences with conjunctions, perhaps in rebellion against all my grade school teachers who marked me off for it. I understand conjunctions are supposed to join ideas together, so it's incorrect to begin with them.

Example 1:

> *I hadn't spoken to him since the incident. And now he wanted to pretend it didn't happen.*

Example 2:

> *It was a simple matter. Done.*
>
> *But I knew there had to be more.*

Used sparingly, this habit of breaking up longer thoughts into smaller sentences, including ones that start with a conjunction, may lend a certain sound and style to your Voice, but when overused, it can become jarring or draw too attention much to the sentences. It's definitely a habit I need to be aware of and break at times during revision so I don't overuse it.

BRIA

One of the things I did constantly when I was a brand new writer was to begin sentences with –ing words. Starting sentences this way was a habit I had a rough time breaking. Considering I didn't even know I was doing it, sometimes I couldn't spot the habit on my own. Honing in on these was a real gift my critique partners had.

Okay, it wasn't quite that bad, but it wasn't pretty. I especially seemed to start paragraphs that way. I'm not sure where the habit began or why it became so prevalent, but it was harder to kick than soda.

Looking back, I found it happening in a couple of typical places. Mostly at the beginning of longer paragraphs and when I wanted to speed up the read. It was a way to make action feel more immediate. More active. A true newbie mistake—one of many on my part.

Basically I was trying to pace my book and using a really cruddy tool.

But once it was pointed out, and I realized what I was trying to do, it allowed me to create better ways to achieve the desired impact.

Being aware of this helped me tremendously. Not only was it something to fix, but it also told me that when I saw a collection of these, I needed to deconstruct my pacing, figure out what the strongest pace for my Core Voice would be, and pull out the correct tools to complete the job. I did not get rid of all of those sentences. Having a diverse sentence structure is important for pace, emphasis, and—let's be honest—to avoid sounding like a lullaby.

From there, I looked at word choice, white space, dialogue, tags, description, setting, how many people I was trying to balance on the page...Well, basically, I looked at everything we've been covering. But this time, it was with a focus on not losing my voice.

Finding one of my Fatal Flaws allowed me not only to fix it, but it forced me to write stronger. Working on the flaw also strengthened several other tools I had in my mental toolbox.

Every Fatal Flaw is an opportunity.

But you might ask, isn't this just finding a way to work around a weakness? Yes...and no.

The weakness was the flaw. You don't want to strengthen a flaw. You want to spot it, kill it, and replace it with something stronger. Basically drop that butter knife you're using to loosen a screw and grab the power screwdriver instead.

BRAIN FLEX

There are a bunch of different Fatal Flaws, but we're going to talk about some of the most common: Sentence Structure Fatal Flaws.

We highly suggest using this tactic to study your work overall and narrow in on some of the other issues you struggle with.

This is a great exercise to do with someone else. Blind spots are always hard to pinpoint on your own—that's why we call them blind spots! But if you're solo and not ready to show your work to other people yet, you can still go on a Fatal Flaws hunt.

Grab a scene you aren't quite happy with. It should be at least two pages because you're going to need enough room to see patterns.

Reading out loud here is a strong tool because your ear will catch things you otherwise wouldn't.

You're also going to need some highlighters or colored pens and your notebook.

Ready? Go!

Read through the two pages.

Does anything jump out immediately? Make a note of it in your notebook. Write down all the issues you spot. Things that stand out might just be a standard writing device you're using on those two pages, so don't rush to any conclusions.

Now go back and look deeper.

But how do you dig deeper? You wrote these words, so they must have seemed good at the time, right?

The first thing we're going to do is highlight every other sentence. This gives you a quick look at sentence length. If all your highlights are about the same length, you should examine that throughout your manuscript.

Now read just the first word of your sentences. If you're seeing a consistent opening word or phrase, that may signal an issue with repeating structure or a different Fatal Flaw.

For example, do all your sentences start with he/she or a name? Red flag on the play! Examine that structure and revise.

In the last step, go through several paragraphs marking the parts of the sentence (such as putting an "SN" over subject-noun and an "N" over other nouns) so you start to see if there's a specific pattern all your sentences fall into. Do they all have the same word pattern? Shake it up!

Remember, you don't want your Core Voice to be a patterned structure that puts people to sleep or makes them want to skim!

One final note on sentence structure: ensure that your grammar skills are strong. That way, if you break a rule, you should be doing it on purpose with purpose.

CHECK IN

How many patterns did you spot? How were they connected?

Hopefully, you used your entire toolbox on these two pages to strengthen them and improve the strength of your writing and the ease of the read.

This is what a first pass read-through should always look like. Look for your weaknesses and fix them with your strengths.

PART VI

ONE VOICE - MULTIPLE VOICES

MULTIPLE CHARACTERS – DIFFERENT VOICES

One common criticism authors deal with, whether it's in a standalone book or an ongoing series is, "All the characters sound the same."

While frustrating, this complaint shouldn't be a surprise. You've spent all this time figuring out what your Voice is and how to use it. Now, the key is to utilize those skills to create more diverse voices within your own overarching Author Voice.

There are several ways to come at this problem, and we're going to tackle them all.

The first is making sure you have a clear Voice for your main character(s).

Your MC (main character) is not you. If your MC is you, you're writing a memoir. If you are writing a memoir, feel free to skip this section. If not...Let's get to it!

Your MC should have clear characteristics of her own that make her real to your readers. She may have some characteristics in common with you. But not all of them. She needs to be a person in her own right for her voice to cut through yours.

This isn't like telling a story about a friend. You aren't performing mimicry. You're digging deeper than that to something closer to channeling. She should be on the page, not you.

We know we're now telling you to get yourself off the page after we just spent numerous sections getting your voice on the page. And this is where the rubber hits the road and leaves a boatload of skid marks. Can you imagine how many skid marks it would take to fill a boat?

We're moving beyond getting your voice on the page. Our goal is to make your voice so deeply ingrained within your writing that it's invisible. So deep that readers know in their hearts what your voice is, but they're not overtly aware of it on any given page. Remember when we talked about not being able to define incredible voices? That's where we're heading now.

Your voice has gone stealth. And this is how it sneaks up on your readers, pulling them into your story and making the characters unforgettable.

Let's deal with this one step at a time.

Whether you're a Plotter or a Pantser, you're going to have to know your characters inside and out. It doesn't matter if they carry the story or if they're a walk-on. Each character needs to possess their own function, personality traits, etc.

The most important of these are your main characters. This could be a protagonist, antagonist, hero, heroine—or any combination of those. But these characters will be the ones to carry your story to its conclusion.

DISCOVERING YOUR CHARACTERS IN PRE-WORK

If you're a high-level planner, you might have done a bunch of pre-work before sitting down to start drafting. Character sketches often including GMC (goal, motivation, conflict), backstory, appearance, and a host of other things. But did you include Voice?

A few character sketch sheets we've seen contain some surface level Voice sections. Things like verbal tics, inner voice cues, key expressions, tone, etc.

These are great starting places, but what makes people sound different?

If you've spent any time with a group of teenage girls lately, you've noticed a cultural phenomenon that has been true since the dawn of teenage girls. When you're speaking to them one-on-one, their personalities shine through clearly. Each girl, while maybe having similarities to her friends, has her own style, inflection, word choice, humor, focus, and interests.

Sure, they're fourteen, and they're all close friends, but separately they're all their own individuals as well.

But get them in a room together and you can watch it happen right before your eyes. Depending on the group, the extent of it can be extreme. The girls begin to tend toward one another, and their distinctive characteristics begin to blend toward a common voice-denominator.

We're not going to get into a deep socio-hierarchical study of teen girl cliques (Bria's pretty sure Jeannie would just make her delete it if she did). But ignoring the inherent leveling that goes on in any group, the pattern is still the same. And while for most people this pattern dissipates somewhere in high school, for others it doesn't.

Which book do you want to write? The one with several uniquely interesting characters or the one with a pack of clones deviated by small degrees?

You'd better pick the right answer.

Depending on the POV of the story, behavior comes through in Voice as much as in dialogue and inner dialogue. How deep your third-person POV is or how telling your first-person POV is will define how much of the Voice you hand over to the POV character.

Starting with your most important characters, answer these questions in-depth about the way your character speaks, thinks, and acts:

- How are her goals and desires demonstrated in how she speaks?
- How does her backstory influence those goals and desires?
- How does her background influence how she thinks?
- What is her world like?
- How does her GMC impact her behavior and levels of motivational desire?

BRIA

After writing books that take place in the nonspecific US Northeast and then writing a book that takes place in what my coastal friends not-so-lovingly refer to as "flyover states," I can tell you that my characters' background impacts how they speak, what they say and when they say it.

Anyone who has spent significant time in other regions of the US comes to understand that regional sayings and cultural cues are far different than how they appear at first glance. For example, people jokingly use the "bless your heart" phrase of the South, but don't truly understand its sliding scale.

When I wrote *Wreckless*, the MC wasn't as far removed from me as people expected. Having grown up dividing time between my father's Boston Irish family and my mother's southern-Midwest family, Bridget felt very much like an extension of myself I didn't get to enjoy enough currently living in Boston.

The ways that the setting and background impacted how Bridget communicated were clear to me. She was in no way a stereotype of a place, but she was definitely someone who had been affected by the world she lived in.

A warning here. Just like with language and dialects, you need to truly understand a place if you're going to immerse your characters deep within your story's setting. The cultural norms of different areas of the US (let alone outside the US) are so numerous, we'd have to write several volumes to scratch the surface.

What we're talking about here is how living in a specific place/region can profoundly shape your character's choices, desires, fears, etc. I can't suggest strongly enough getting a beta reader from your book's setting if it's not a location you're deeply in tune with.

Also, maps and Google are great. But they won't tell you that Massachusetts locals don't call it the Yankee Division Highway, even though that's what you'll see on the map. They simply call it 128.

The examples of localisms are numerous for every setting.

These aren't Voice issues, but they're just as important to understand—not only because you as an author should get them right, but because your character needs to so she has credibility. When she says, "I'm taking the red line out to Brookline" she just lost all the locals...unless she's lost, and then we're in on the joke.

Keep Voice solid by not losing your character's credibility.

If you're curious about regionalisms and linguistic structure, I can't recommend Deborah Tannen's work enough. She's an excellent starting point for linguistics studies. She also has an amazing book about the relational dynamics between mothers and daughters that is a great source for conflict between characters.

As we discussed, one of the benefits of writing characters who have been preplanned is that most of the character details have already been defined, and your focus is on working through the outlined story step by step. With these things in place, you can focus on the craft of the piece to make sure those traits come out in Voice.

DISCOVERING YOUR CHARACTERS IN RE-WORK

BRIA

Pantsers are all looking at us like we're nuts at this point. And I know how they feel. I've gone to innumerable conferences and workshops and picked up book after book to gain a writing tool, only to find out that if I'm not doing a lot of pre-work (otherwise known as plotting), the tools won't work for me. It's a frustration I know a lot of Pantsers feel.

Part of the joy of writing for most Pantsers is the discovery of the characters as you go. With that in mind, how do you balance the journey of self-discovery with the need for creating clear character voices?

For many Pantsers, this is a more natural process. As you write, the characters reveal themselves. This organic process allows the characters to come alive on the page as you write. An advantage

Pantsers have is knowing the majority of the work will be in the edits. This gives them the comfort to move forward, creating the characters and knowing they'll be fine-tuned during the editing phase. (Jeannie: Ahem, Plotter here, and I also know the majority of my work is in edits. *winks*)

The problem then becomes consistency. It's vital we show growth and change over our characters' arcs without creating a choppy growth where suddenly the character feels like someone else...even if that someone else is finally a fully fleshed-out character.

One suggestion is to create an Ah-Ha Sheet.

If you're anything like us, you think you're going to remember everything. That once something has been added it will become a constant and you'll be able to slip it in as you do the next read-through.

And this happens...sometimes.

Let's not leave these important character-shaping traits out till our beta readers call us out for inconsistency.

The best way to make the most of your Ah-Ha Sheet will differ for everyone, but here's what I've found works.

There's no need to do a lot of up-front work—we know how most Pantsers hate that.

At the top of the page, make a column for each of the following:

- Character name
- Update
- Page Number
- Quote

A Quote? What's up with that? During editing, pages change. Even chapters change. Being able to search your manuscript using a quote snippet makes the process easier. Also, seeing the change in action will be helpful when you're at a loss to remember everything during revisions. The Find tool in Microsoft Word is indispensable for this.

I suggest doing this digitally so you can group characters' updates together.

Why not use comment bubbles instead?

Great question! I'm glad you asked.

We're a huge believer in comments. They help you to visually, spatially, and logically track and change things. They also can be used for a running conversation with yourself about things you want to consider revising in specific sections. But when you get to the end of your read-through, an Ah-Ha Sheet will do several things that using the comment bubbles won't.

First off, it will let you see all the changes in one place. The advantage of this is consistency. Do all the elements combined create the character voice you're looking for? Did you make a decision on characterization and negate it later in the story?

Second, it means nothing will fall through the cracks. Having the change marked where it happens isn't going to do you any good if you don't remember it until you get to it again.

Finally, it will make sure your characters are individuals. If you see that you have more than one character doing the same tics or tones or expressions, you can catch it here in the Ah-Ha Sheet instead of when a beta says to you, "Bria, everyone in this book calls her sweetheart when they're humoring her." (True story.)

BRAIN FLEX

Grab some early pages your main character is active on. Highlight where you feel the character's voice is coming through. Using what we've learned about voice and style (tone, cadence, pacing, literary devices, word choice, quirks, etc.), identify what makes the main character stand out. How is he or she different than the other characters on the page?

CHECK IN

Did you find them? If so, great!

Write your examples down to make sure you have a touchstone for your character's voice to ensure it stays consistent throughout the book.

Didn't find any instances of a distinctive character voice? Time to stop and rethink how your character is making an impression (or not) on the page.

BRAIN FLEX—FOR THE BRAIN FLEX

Make a list of things you expected to find on the page about your character.

What are the things you wanted readers to see about your main character?

Knowing you didn't find that on the page, let's run through some quick questions.

Does she speak quickly? Does she use long sentences? Short? Is she demanding? Does she tiptoe around her points or go right after them?

What's her emotional core for communicating? Humor? Sarcasm? Seriousness? Does she express a strong opinion in the passage? Does she verbalize or internalize it? Why?

CHECK IN

Still struggling with your character's voice?

Turn back to the various exercises you've been doing for yourself and apply your ah-ha moments from each to your main characters.

You can see that those same techniques will help you hone your characters' voices, making them unique and fresh while still feeling like you.

SECONDARY CHARACTERS

So you've firmed up the Voice for each of your main characters. Obviously the people who carry the story are the most important. But what about your secondary characters?

While you may feel the impulse to consider your secondaries as set dressing, that inclination is where you'll go astray and miss out on using your Voice tools to their max.

There are several reasons secondary characters' voices are important:
- Flavor
- Follow-up
- Ability to highlight some characteristic or provide information about the MC
- Ability to say things the MC can't

Secondary characters do more than just give the main character a richer world. Think about meeting a new person. You can tell a lot about her by the company she keeps. Is her best friend snarky, sweet, patient, or a complete idiot? Does she kick puppies while she walks down the street smoking stolen cigars?

And what does this say about your MC? Does it show you she's patient? Loyal? A secret pushover?

Together the MC and her friends create a unit. What do you know about your MC based on her unit?

Don't believe us? How often is Taylor Swift's Girl Squad in the news? How often do articles draw an assumption about the singer and her friends based on who is in the Squad?

That's what your secondaries should be doing for your main character.

If you don't have a clear view of the secondary characters going in—or you've written the book and can't nail down the secondary characters' purpose—asking yourself what their role is in the MC's life is a great place to start.

BRIA

Another key purpose of the secondary characters is adding flavor to the book. One of my struggles has been to not allow my secondary characters to take over the story.

In my Brew Ha Ha series, I have a café barista who tells it like it is. She's snarky, direct, has no boundaries, and is basically the Oracle of the Brew. She's the person who says what everyone else wants to say. You're being annoying or stupid or naïve or close-minded? Don't think you can walk into The Brew and not be called out on it by Abby the Barista.

She forces issues that the other characters are avoiding. She says those things we've all had to bite our tongues to keep back in order to be polite. She moves the story forward.

People love her.

While my heroes are always a hit, in my Brew series, it's Abby who people ask about getting her own story.

The balance is to make sure she's interesting enough and does her job (to keep the story moving forward when the main character doesn't have the power to deal with an issue directly), but without taking over.

It's a balancing act.

Which brings us to another secondary character issue: The Series.

CHARACTERS IN A SERIES

Often we don't know up front if we're writing a series, let alone who will get a book (fellow Pantsers, I'm looking at you).

Our suggestion? Write every character like they'll get a book.

You may not know that going into the story. You may not know that for several books. That's why it's important that every secondary character is fleshed out well.

The key is to create them in a way that is true to their character while allowing them to do the job you hired them to do in the current book.

There is nothing worse than getting to know a secondary character for several books only to have her magically have a personality transplant when she gets her own book.

Most of this characterization is done through Voice.

The secondary characters (who don't have full subplots) shouldn't have enough action or arc to be able to accomplish all the things we just discussed. The only way those things are really constructed is through Voice.

Remember the exercises we just did for the main characters? A quick look at the highlights of your secondaries with those points in mind will tell you if they're doing their jobs or not.

You've created fleshed out characters who are (almost) main characters in their own right...in your head. We've talked about creating them, using them, and making sure they don't take over the story. But how do you do that? How do you balance all of those things? You reduce them down to their core traits. Are they funny or caring or sarcastic or smart or driven?

If you've already written the book, keep these two to three core traits at the front of your mind when editing your secondary character. Remember, a secondary character can't be all things to all people. They have a role, and they need to stay in it while still appearing to be as fleshed out as your main characters.

Think of them as Scotch tape, not duct tape. They can do a couple things really well, but they can't do it all.

I actually have a note card for each secondary character with their core traits. When doing my read-throughs, if the secondary character steps outside her role/personality/voice, I ask myself the following questions:

- Does this need to happen? If so, why is she the character doing it? Is it placed on the right supporting character?
- Is this truly a better core trait? As a character becomes clearer, maybe her voice has as well and the fact is that I need to reconsider her actual traits and role.

BRAIN FLEX

With all that you've learned, we're going to create the Secondary Characters' Core Trait cards.

Make a list of everyone in your book. Yes, even walk-ons. You should know how many of those you have so you can combine them or shift their weight to a secondary wherever possible.

Now make a card for everyone who is Secondary in this book or this series.

The card should have the following:
- Character name
- Brief character description (you're going to want that later)
- Two or three key character traits. No more
- Any key sayings or personality quirks

Nothing else. That's it. And that's where your secondary character without a subplot/arc should live.

Now go through the cards, and do a search in your manuscript for each of them. Read the pages where the secondary character has screen time and ensure you have continuity of voice and arc.

CHECK IN

Did the secondary character's traits match the card? Did you have to shift the character's voice, description, or actions on any of your pages...or the card? Were each what you expected?

This is the time to focus on just the secondary.

SO YOU'VE DONE THE WORK

Now the core traits for the characters have been defined and checked. Each character is his or her own person. Great! But how do they all come together?

This isn't just about the characters as individuals. It's about balance in your story.

This brings us back to the principle issue: How do you make sure each character doesn't just sound different, but is different?

Pull out your Core Traits cards. Is there a lot of overlap? Sure, friends are similar, but they aren't the same. If the core traits overlap too much, you should probably reconsider and dive back into evaluating the traits of each and figuring out who the secondary characters truly are.

It should be clear during a read-through which character is which. If you come across a passage where you're not sure how a character would speak, then ask yourself if you really are clear on what each secondary character is like.

If you want to see this in action and done incredibly well, I highly recommend reading *Bet Me* by Jennifer Crusie.

This book contains two sets of friends—three guys and three girls. On top of the two main characters and their two best friends, there are also three other secondary characters and about nine other main walk-on characters. At any given time there are one to nine people on the page. Crusie balances the distinctive character voices so well that you're able to follow the scene without ever confusing one character's dialogue or action with another's.

Another Jennifer Crusie book that shows an amazing number of characters balanced on the page is Maybe This Time. This book's cast of characters isn't a group of friends, so the differences are even more distinct. All the characters are distinguishable while remaining within the scope of what their job is. Crusie does an amazing job of providing clear voices for all her characters—so much so that she uses far fewer identification tags than a less experienced writer would need to balance that many people on the page.

A Note: We looked for an example that would make this premise clear and found that even the greats leave scenes like this till later in the book. The slow build of voice and characterization means that when read out of context, clarity is lost.

They develop the main characters' voices so strongly you can never be in doubt of who they are. Then, as the secondary and minor characters join them on the page, they give them their own smaller roles and personalities to make this work.

It's a build—low, strong, and subtle, but there and solid.

BRIA

My first book was this huge fantasy. It was the first of a five-book series. It had the hero and heroine...plus six other important characters, several of whom had POV scenes.

I actually did a read for each secondary character. How? I'd do a Find/Replace for her name. Then I'd go to each of her scenes and read only her dialogue...and move on to the next scene. Doing this I got to hear the consistency—or lack thereof—in each of the characters' voices.

It was one of the best things I did for my secondaries with a book that large.

BRAIN FLEX

Do you have the right secondary characters? What is their purpose?

Grab your cards! They're updated, cleaned up, and accurate. They're going to let you look at everyone at once. Use them to ask yourself the following questions:

- Is everyone different?
- Do some characters seem too similar?
- Does each one have a job or purpose within the story?
- Do the jobs overlap?
- Are there too many/not enough people to make these character and story arcs work?

CHECK IN

Once you've considered the previous questions, there are some follow-up questions to address any potential issues. Do you have overlap between characters? Should two or more of those characters be combined? Is the character not getting her job done now that you know what it is? Are the character traits consistent with the job? Do they remain the same or have a small (read: appropriate for a secondary character without a subplot) arc?

This is the perfect time to guarantee you have all your ducks in a row and ensure your characters are consistent. Is your character only fulfilling a single purpose in that scene with no other justification for her inclusion in the story?

This is a great question and a common problem. If that is the case, the secondary becomes a device, not a character. As an issue, it may feel small. The character seems consistent and works independently in each scene, but does she stand up under scrutiny?

Trust us, you're going to have readers who reread your books. When I hear that, I'm curious what they're seeing that they didn't see in their first...or second...read. The devil is in the details, and often those details are in your secondary characters.

BRIA

I just had an e-mail from a reader telling me she'd read my latest book for the ninth time.

Nine.

Seriously. That's more than my critique partners have read it.

But she sent me a list of things she noticed on this read she hadn't noticed before. Little details about the hero and heroine, but she also caught some things about the secondaries that would be important later. Not quite Easter eggs, but things so subtle they made the characters "real" without making them stereotypes. She asked questions I couldn't answer without spoilers.

She got it.

She got it because the details were there thanks to my focus on the characters' Core Traits.

Let's make sure they're seeing the right thing before they spot that inconsistency we were hoping to brush under the rug.

PART VII

DEVELOPING YOUR SIGNATURE VOICE

WELCOME TO THE REST OF THE BATTLE

We've come a long way.

You should definitely take a moment and think about where you were at the beginning of this book. You weren't sure where your voice stood or where you wanted to go. You may not have even known if you had a Voice.

We've talked about writing with the basic building blocks way back down at Emerging Voice. We've taken those building blocks and built them into something strong: a Core Voice that would get us attention and probably even a shot at an agent or a contract.

We've differentiated the levels of Voice into Emerging, Core, and Signature, because only when you have a strong foundation in your Core Voice do you have the tools and direction to know where you want to head.

We've moved from having a general direction (how to improve our voices) to a specific point on the horizon of what we want our Voices to sound like. Only you can know where you want to take your voice next. Only you can define what it means to strive for your Signature Voice.

Core Voice is nothing to sneeze at. Most authors live on the Core Voice level for the majority of their careers. It's a strong place to live. It's definitely the Big Time.

But why stop there? This is a book dedicated to Finding Your Voice. We'd be stopping short if we didn't address the final step. Developing a Signature Voice means pushing beyond, aspiring not only to have a strong, memorable Voice, but a Voice that will break you out from the pack.

BRIA

I want to be a Go-To Author.

Who doesn't?

But do you know what that means for you? I want to be the Go-To Author for fun, quirky stories with a richness to them. When people are looking for that, I want readers to say, "Oh, have you tried Bria Quinlan?"

SIGNATURE VOICE: THE GAME CHANGER

Authors spend a significant amount of time discovering their Core Voice and, once they've found it, they further develop it until it becomes second nature. Authors who have made this leap live in their Core Voice and use it to attract readers and build a brand. You can be successful once you've developed your Core Voice. Readers will come back to read you again and again. You're not just putting a story on the page, you're telling it and telling it well.

You've succeeded in "Finding Your Voice and Making it Heard" as this book's title promises.

So what's this next level called Signature Voice?

By showing you there's another level, we're saying the game doesn't end there. It doesn't end there because we want more.

As authors who love craft, we strive to grow stronger with each book. When it comes to honing a Core Voice into a Signature Voice, the path becomes even more elusive because only you can define your path and goals.

At this point we Owls have to make a confession: we're still shaping our Signature Voices. We're playing with our craft and making the climb to the next level: a breakthrough book. Significant growth in our exposure and audience. We want to become a household name in our respective genres. Dream big, right?

We know a lot of the breakout success we've just described depends on luck and timing. But as Owls who love craft, we also believe there is one huge component of the path we do control. That part is our storytelling ability and effectiveness as communicators and entertainers. Achieving the higher level of ability is what fuels this last part of the Voice journey.

This is why we say your Signature Voice will change. As you create new stories and experiment with new elements and genres, your Signature Voice will reflect your approach toward that genre or story. The goal is to reach a point where your unique voice intertwines with your story in such a way that they elevate one another to create a standout, unforgettable read. Your Signature Voice will stay in your readers' minds and hearts and make them come back for more.

WHAT DOES IT MEAN TO DEVELOP YOUR SIGNATURE VOICE?

JEANNIE

Looking back, it feels like I discovered what my Core Voice was around my third manuscript (before I was published), and then spent the next nine books developing it into a Signature Voice. And I'm still developing it.

What that means for me is that when I write a rough draft now, it does sound distinctively like me. All of the foundational elements are there: word choice, sentence structure, cadence, etc. Sure, it's still a rough draft, but my Core Voice is recognizable in the first pass without my having to think too hard about it. The work I find myself doing is enhancing my voice by stripping away deadweight in the manuscript and focusing on specific parts of the story I want to amp up, such as the emotional context and worldbuilding.

This doesn't mean that I do fewer line edits. I'm still going down the lines, scratching out words and sentences and writing little "do better" notes where I should have challenged myself more. There's still a lot of work. But the Voice part does get easier. Mainly because I know my process better, and I know what I want out of it.

Now that I know the things I do well and enjoy doing, I want to use that to grow my Signature Voice. I strive to create memorable scenes and stories that stay with the reader long after they've closed the book. I want to be an author that readers will seek out and not be able to put down.

BRIA

Adding to what Jeannie said about finding her Core Voice and shaping her Signature Voice, I feel like my aim as a writer is clearer now. I no longer have to figure out how to tell a story. I know the Voice I'm aiming for. I know that I'm going to be shaping that Core Voice and getting it even sharper over time.

While it's a focus, it feels less heavy on my author shoulders because I understand my path now.

IDENTIFYING YOUR SWEET SPOT

BRIA

Everyone has a sweet spot for what they specialize in. For me, writing humor is all about finding it.

The essence of the phrase "sweet spot" leaves you thinking about finding that middle ground. But that's not always true. Sometimes it's going too far. Or understating. Or completely ignoring.

The best part about sweet spots is they aren't all the same. This isn't like golf where everyone has to get that same little ball in that tiny hole on the other side of a huge field. Your sweet spot, the one that works for you, isn't going to work for me.

Usually when my CPs tell me a joke fell flat (and it's a universal agreement), they'll throw out other potential punch lines. The thing is, nine times out of ten, none those work for me. But they may trigger something that is my voice...is my sweet spot.

For me, humor is about "how far?" How far is too far? How far pushes the limits of ridiculousness? While my stories can be a bit over-the-top—rompy—they're actually fairly reality-solid. The over-the-top part of over-the-top won't work for me. The story and characters still have to stay grounded.

For example, if you're one of my readers, you'll remember a scene in *Wreckless* where Bridget and the girls talk about setting something on fire. I wrote that giggling to myself the entire time, and thinking, this is going to be too far for Bridget. She's way too serious.

But every time I did a read-through, I couldn't bring myself to cut it. It made me laugh each time. It's one of the most commented scenes in my YAs (the other one being when I almost kill someone, so...yeah).

Back when indie publishing was new, R. L. Mathewson hit the scene pretty early with her Neighbors from Hell series. She didn't even have covers (they were just the title and her name), but her blurb grabbed me, so I grabbed her book. She's still a reread for me. I couldn't pull off her level of over-the-top in my stories, but she does it brilliantly. Her sweet spot is further out than mine.

And it works. She knows exactly where it is. Every time I think she's going to go too far, that her style and voice are leading me to something that I'll roll my eyes at, she swings that scene in a new direction and nails it. That's knowing how to use your voice to complement your style and story.

I find that, because my Signature Voice and my rompy comedy are more understated or dry, I fill my Disaster Draft with comments like "Go further," "This isn't funny enough...or at all," or "What's bigger than this?"

I had to learn to leave the fear of going too far, too big, or too funny, behind. When you know where your Signature Voice sits, your next step is figuring out if it's easy to push into it or pull back to it.

For me, it's better to push as far as I can in drafts, and then, when push comes to shove, rein it back in if it's too far.

It's almost never too far, and once I accepted that, drafting in my Signature Voice became much easier and helped me to have easier rounds of editing and revising.

JEANNIE

When I was revising my second novel, *The Dragon and the Pearl*, my editor and I went through five rounds. She wanted a little more emotion from the hero. I thought it would ruin his entire core nature, so I would only give in inches at a time. I'd get a new round of notes: "Better, but more on the hero's motivation." Another inch. More notes...and so on.

Then she finally called me up, and we had a talk about Chinese film and storytelling and how there was a very distant feel to it, as if it was rude to take too close of a look at these characters. That's when I had a lightbulb moment. There was a certain degree of distance in my storytelling voice, put there by choice, yet I was writing in a genre where the reader is brought in very close and expects to see all the characters' emotions, thoughts, and motivations—if not at the beginning, then by the end of the story.

For me, that sweet spot is riding the line of restraint and emotion. I don't want to give anything away too easily, but when I do let the reader in, I want the payoff to be worth it. The slow build is something I seem to be able to hit frequently. The restraint in my Signature Voice lends itself to that simmering level of emotion. What I focus on is where the emotion breaks through, to ensure it happens in a believable and satisfactory way.

Whenever I'm getting editorial notes, I pay careful attention to the ones about motivation throughout the book. In revisions, I'm trying to push far enough that the emotional dots all get connected and the character motivations aren't so mysterious. I spend extra passes going over the emotional high points of the book, adding additional context and detail on each pass.

You're at the point that you know your Core Voice, and you're starting to look up the slope toward Signature Voice. Key elements of our voices are humor and character motivation, but you may find the key factor that you need to rein in or build up is something completely different. Now is the time to discover what your voice's major Signature component is so you can hone and develop it.

The only way to find that special It Factor is to discover it for yourself. Once you've established your Core Voice, you'll recognize your strengths and weaknesses, and you'll also have the tools to experiment. You can play with your boundaries and make tweaks to your voice without imitating someone else's style. You'll be able to operate from a solid base that is wholly and uniquely YOU.

BRAIN FLEX

Are you a "go big" or understated writer? Do you know what your voice lends itself to for emphasis when you need it?

Take an unedited scene from your manuscript.

Keeping in mind that you are looking to enhance Core Voice, take a highlighter and highlight your Voice's key component in the scene. This can be an emotional point or important detail where you've placed special emphasis. It might be a snappy piece of dialogue that really brings out your characterizations.

CHECK IN

Are you hitting the points properly? Does the scene have the impact that you intend it to?

If not, have you gone too far or not far enough? What does your Core Voice instinctually tell you to do here?

Do it.

GOING TOO FAR

As mentioned in the previous section, sometimes the answer is to keep on pushing. But what happens if you've gone past your sweet spot, and you're now melodramatic instead of emotional? Corny instead of funny? You're trying too hard, and it shows on the page. It's the equivalent of speaking a little too fast and too loud at a party when you're trying to impress someone.

In general, you don't need to worry about this while drafting or revising...If anything, you should always be pushing your own boundaries. A good bit of advice from author Linda Howard is that if you go too far, someone can always pull you back. But if you don't go far enough, no one will be able to tell you how to get there. It's very difficult for someone to tell you what's missing.

(JEANNIE here: It's difficult for someone to tell you what's missing unless you have someone who is familiar with your voice, like Bria, who has been known to leave notes on my manuscript like, "Make this sound more like Jeannie Lin.")

So in the beginning, push on forward. Don't fear.

But now we're nearing the end...at least of this book. What happens if you've reached the point where your prose is overwritten and overworked? What if you can't tell anymore?

This is where having tough love readers that you trust will help. And it's also good to get readers who are not familiar with your work so they can tell you if these little quirks you consider part of your Core Voice are distracting and taking the reader out of the story.

Sometimes overwritten prose isn't a matter of voice, but more a lack of direction. It's writing for writing's sake. An example of this is overuse of big, complex words for the sake of using big, complex words. We all did this in essays for English class, right? *raises hand* If the words aren't chosen for power or purpose, they start to have the opposite effect.

Similarly, sentence fragments are frequently used to create a disjointed, staccato effect to draw attention. When overused, the purpose gets lost.

"He took a sip. It was cold. Cold and bitter. As bitter as denial."

This once cool device can become distracting. Readers are paying attention to the writing—and not in a good way—instead of the story.

BRAIN FLEX

Put the pages that you're working on away. Do it for at least two weeks. No. I'm not kidding. During that time, journal. When you aren't working on your work, and you're only thinking about craft, you reach a different place. It stops being about the words right in front of you right now. And more about your big picture.

We've looked at Voice in chunks. We've even threaded some of those chunks together. But if you step away, far away, it's like any picture. You're seeing the whole instead of the details alone.

When you come back to it, read it out loud to yourself or have someone read it to you. If anything sounds awkward or forced, mark it for revision.

GET A LITTLE HELP

Writers are often surrounded by other writers who will never be able to read like just a reader again. Find a reader who is willing to read through your chapter and only mark the spots where they felt pulled out of the story. They don't have to explain why. They just have to mark the spots that made them pause or stop or reread for any reason. For each of those spots, examine them and figure out what might be the problem. It might be something, a plot point or character motivation, which needed to be cleared up. Or it might be writing that needs to be cleaned up.

PART VIII

VOICE IN PROCESS FOR PANTSERS & PLOTTERS

HOLDING ONTO YOUR VOICE

Okay, we know you thought you were done...but not so fast!

You worked hard to narrow down your voice, define it, create a solid Core Voice that will sell and are working your way up the incline toward a Signature Voice that will make you rich and famous (or something like that). What could possibly be left?

There is one other topic that's important. One that's so broad it could be overwhelming: holding on to your voice throughout your writing process.

We often get questions about what the process of developing and enhancing your Voice actually looks like in practice. Now we can't speak to every process. Everyone's process is different—as it should be.

Imagine a long line diagram with "Plotter" at one end and "Pantser" at the other. Almost no one sits on those far ends of the spectrum. Each person tends to favor one end or the other.

Speaking in absolutes about being a Pantser or a Plotter can be more confusing than helpful. Instead, we'll each discuss how we not only hold on to our voices but shape them during the writing process.

INSIDE THE MIND OF A PANTSER

BRIA

I'm a Pantser and a pretty hardcore one at that. I sit wayyyyyy down the spectrum at the "writing into the mist" end. There's basically zero pre-work for me. An idea starts me thinking, which starts me writing—and who knows where I'll end up from there!

It took me a long time to use this as my greatest asset for my voice. To do this, I have to give myself permission to do a lot of things.

Write stuff I'll throw away.
Write tangents.
Write ridiculous.
Go over the top.
Be boring.

All of these things can be fixed in revisions and edits. Let's look at why granting myself permission to write badly made my work stronger...and how it can make your work stronger too.

PERMISSION TO THROW STUFF AWAY

Sometimes knowing things are going to get deleted makes moving on easier. I throw away at least 10 percent of what I think I'm going to keep. Sometimes the reason is that it misses the mark on my voice.

Why is this a helpful way to hold on to your voice? If you're focusing on writing only things you're going to keep, you may get stuck in the world of perfecting the first draft. For a far-end Pantser like me, being dragged to a halt by things like word choice in my Disaster Draft would kill my flow.

The first thing I do is work on the near impossible chore of turning off my internal editor. This does a lot of things for me.

By giving myself permission to delete everything I write before I've even written it, I've turned off the fear of "losing words" later and allowed my internal editor to go on deleting-hiatus in the drafting phase. This means, perfection is off the table while drafting—and we (me and that pesky little voice) both know that.

Voice is only one part. Story, conflict, flow, arcs, etc., also contribute. By saying, "This may get thrown out, and that's okay," I'm able to move past the spot that's worrying me and continue with getting the story on the page.

This allows me to go places I may cut in the next two read-throughs.

REVISIONS

Revision can be tricky. You never know how much is going to happen during the process. If you're changing a significant story or character arc, it's important to make sure you're consistent with those changes throughout the manuscript. If any updates impact character voice, revise accordingly. Voice (both yours and the characters') needs to be considered intrinsically part of your arcs.

This is one of the reasons I have my Ah-Ha Sheet. It keeps track of my characters, their arcs, their voice tics, etc. Having that allows me to enter this phase confident that I'm making things better—not mucking them up spot-reading.

So the book is done, revised, and ready to be edited.

Working with an editor can really catch those last-minute Voice issues.

My beta readers have said straight out to me on occasion, "that character would not say that." Most of the time, they're right. This is a great chance to have a second or third set of eyes on the story to make sure that your character's voice stays true.

If your voice is still something you're not feeling confident about, add it to the list of questions for your beta readers.

Do you feel like the character has a clear voice? Do you feel that the character's dialogue is true to the character throughout the read? Is there any time when you felt as though her words weren't true to her overall character voice?

Examining these issues will help you in those last edits to make sure all your hard work pays off on the final page.

The first draft is just to get the words on the page, but after that I'm looking for clarity and consistency. Working in chunks can get me far. I'll up my humor, check my scenes, grow my characters, hit my emotional and turning points harder, add in some hidden jokes my readers will find on a second or third read, etc.

But working in chunks doesn't guarantee I have the consistency I want.

For that reason, I make a list of things to check—including Voice—on a last read-through before it gets to the final edits.

Checking Voice is on that list.

This isn't something that will happen by accident. Ensuring my voice—and the character voices—are all solidly where I want them means work. It means purposefully revising for voice during that last read. It means being aware. It means being willing to listen to my betas when they say, "Something doesn't sound right here," and knowing it's probably Voice.

As someone who is almost a straight Pantser, I go into the drafting process with a basic idea. A very basic idea. It usually includes some knowledge about the hero and heroine and, maybe—if I'm lucky—the black moment. Any ideas of what the story is or how it will unfold occur organically during the first Disaster Draft.

Granted, this means I often have huge additions to the first draft (especially in the first ten to fifteen pages), but that's what works for me.

No matter where your process is on the sliding scale between Pantser and Plotter, you need to be certain of a couple things:
- You know what your process is
- You understand how to use it
- It works for you

Each process is going to be different—and have inherently different issues to contend with. Don't let others define your process. Find it, refine it, and work it.

Now, let's look at the other end of the spectrum.

INSIDE THE MIND OF A PLOTTER

JEANNIE

On the scale of Pantser to Plotter, I would consider myself smack in the middle of the Plotter camp. I don't do a lot of pre-work when it comes to the characters. Once, when a blogger asked me to do a character interview, I practically broke out in hives. My characters don't talk to me, and I sure as heck don't talk back.

Where I concentrate my planning work is my plot outline. I lay out the major events and places where turning points need to occur, but I don't necessarily flesh out every scene.

My process starts with one seed—a central idea. If the idea is not strong enough, it never takes root. But once that idea starts sprouting, I commit to it. As one of my critique partners points out: I date one idea at a time for the most part.

The first step in my process is a brainstorm. Sometimes I do this with other writers. We'll sit in a room and spitball the concept by throwing out a bunch of ideas. Most of the time, it's all in my head. I pull out fragments of plot as I'm driving, or the moment before I fall asleep, or while I'm on long conference calls. Or sometimes I pace around in circles with a blank look on my face.

This is probably more than you need to know about me. Or maybe this description is really singing to you, and you're saying, Yes! That's totally me!

From the brainstorm sessions, certain scenes start to gain favor. Usually one of these is how the book opens. The other scenes tend to be turning points, those high drama scenes that come out so vividly in your head. The ones you can't wait to write. I had the fabulous Li Bai Shen's scenes from *My Fair Concubine* in my head for a good year before I ever wrote a single word down.

When I feel there are enough of these turning points to anchor the story, I sit down to write an outline. This is why I call myself an incubator. Before my plotting process even begins, I've been keeping the idea warm under my wing for a while.

The outline is plotted to roughly two structures: The basic three-act structure for screenplays, which is sometimes broken down further as a six-act structure, and Christopher Vogler's *The Writer's Journey: Mythic Structure for Writers*. The six-act structure is the method I use for placing turning points in my plot outline. It's not uncommon for me to write, "Hero discovers something unexpected about the heroine here" in the outline when I know that I want a turning point in that chapter, but I don't know what that big reveal will be yet.

I also lay the hero's journey steps over the six-act structure in order to fine-tune the events that will occur at the turning points.

In addition to these two methods, I also plot according to theme. During the planning phase, I already have an idea of the broad themes of the story and use those to make decisions when determining what the main conflict as well as secondary storylines should be.

I go over the outline a few times, but I don't fret if there are some foggy parts. Then I name the characters if they don't yet have a name. My outline runs about twenty-one to twenty-four chapters. Why so rigid? This is my process and the one I trust. It's not that I have to end up at twenty-four chapters, but if I write out an entire plot outline and can only fill seventeen chapters, that's a red flag for me. I don't have enough substance to the story, which is going to come back and bite me later.

I think that's the core of my Plotter identity. As a Plotter, I need a roadmap, but it's not the whats and hows and whys of the plot that serve as my roadmap; I'm fairly comfortable with filling in more plot details as I start writing. Having my process in place is what acts as my guide and security blanket, but that process undeniably revolves around planning and refining the plot.

Once I have my outline and protagonists' names down, I'm ready to write out the first pages of the story. Wow, looking back, that's a lot of work before ever writing one word. Maybe I need to push my needle a little further over into the Plotter camp.

When I start a manuscript, I write out the entire first chapter, and then pause to get a feel for how things are working and if the story is coming out as I envisioned. I don't do significant revisions at this stage. My process has evolved to the point where I expect the very first part of the book to change once I'm all the way through. Even if the scene and events don't change much, I will still layer in connections to the larger theme and/or character arcs. At the end, I will always loop back so that the beginning and ending scene somehow reference each other if they don't already. This is so I can layer in a sense of purpose at the beginning as well as a sense of closure at the end.

DRAFTING

Then, with opening and outline in hand, I start fast drafting. Ideally, I write the first version of the book in about three to four weeks in a very fast and ugly draft. If I'm moving slowly, this can take four to six weeks.

During the fast draft, I care very little about Voice. I care more about getting the tension and structural rising and falling actions in place. I have found, over time, that my voice does come out more naturally in the early draft, but there are a lot of rough spots around it.

After I hit a very rocky "The End," I take two or three days to think on it, now that I can envision the book from start to finish. My next pass ties the story together in what I call a "human consumable" draft. This means gaps like "finish this scene later" are filled in so the read makes some sense from point A to point B.

During this pass, I do make an attempt to take the "easy" steps toward enhancing my voice. By this I mean I delete a lot of deadweight. I make very little attempt to polish.

By the end, I have a workable draft, but it's still really ugly. So ugly only a mother can love it.

At this point, I bravely send it to Bria and a few trusted readers.

REVISIONS

If my ugly draft manuscript comes back with very few comments, I seek more advice. I expect feedback at this point to be bloody. I welcome it. By nature, I'm a person who likes to troubleshoot and debug. If I have no comments, I have no direction.

As much as I welcome all advice, the feedback I take with a grain of salt is line edits. I discard most grammatical fixes and line edits at this phase. The manuscript is not ready for that type of polish. It's too early to start layering in Voice because there are still drastic changes to be done here. I'll just end up breaking everything again.

At this stage, I work on structural and character edits, but as the problem areas are smoothed out, I can see what the final version will look like. After the major revisions are complete, I do a cleaning pass where I do start looking at the actual words on the page and pay attention to the cadence and flow of the writing. Here is where I look at chapters and scenes and balancing out elements like dialogue and narration. I check my pacing and shape the story into what the composition will be in the final version. My voice is recognizable after this process, but it still has a lot of rough edges.

AND MORE REVISIONS

Bria has remarked several times to me that I start big and whittle down. Nowhere is this more evident than in my revision process.

I'm now ready for a revision to enhance Voice and polish the manuscript. This is the hardest revision for me. At this point, I know the story, including its themes; high and low points; turning points; and opening and ending. This is the pass where I angst about word choice and fixing sentences. It's no longer about story, but about readability.

Then I do one last pass. I hit the opening and the closing once more to make sure all the right moments are highlighted. The opening gets more attention than the closing in terms of Voice. It's where the reader will decide to come along with me or close the book.

ON TO THE PROFESSIONALS

Regardless of whether I'm independently publishing or traditionally publishing, my manuscript will go through professional line and copy edits. I'm mentioning this because this is where I find myself protecting my voice. If an editor is rewriting your sentences at this stage—it's a warning flag.

If you've done the work and you know your voice, defend your choices! There's a little give and take in terms of correcting grammar and awkward sentences. But your name is on the cover; these are your words. The red warning light comes on if there's any major attempt to edit my lines. There rarely is, but the moment a line editor changes my sentences, I know it. Even if it's not marked up, I can tell if I didn't write something.

Up until this point, I've been willing to make sweeping changes in the manuscript. There's very little I'll refuse to revise if I find the feedback worthwhile. But now, when I've made my decisions, I fight like a tigress to preserve my voice.

FINAL STAGE

At some point during final galleys, I'll find myself changing the same sentences back and forth. Tweaking single words that I know no reader would really notice but for some reason drive me crazy. This is when I have to slap my own hand away and let it go. This is hard for me. The first words out of my mouth when I held my first published book in my hands? "Now I can't fix it anymore."

So, yes. Know your own crazy. There's no such thing as perfection. Let it go.

BRINGING IT ALL TOGETHER
IS IT WORKING?

Looking back, you've got a notebook full of notes, manuscript pages full of changes, and a list of questions to keep asking yourself. That's a lot. But how do you bring it all together?

We understand tackling this many things at once can be overwhelming. And, if we're doing it right, it should be. Every writer wants to grow, wants to become a better teller of stories.

To do this, knowing how you work is important...and we're not talking about your Plotter vs Pantser tendencies this time. We're talking about how you actually work. We suggest looking at the exercises, running through them and their outcomes again quickly.

Where did you have the biggest ah-ha moment? Which one seemed like the easiest one to implement in your day-to-day work? Was there one that really struck a chord with you that's going to need some steady study to make a difference?

The point is that just doing the exercise isn't going to change your writing. It's going to make you aware of your writing, where you can improve, and give you ideas on how to begin that process.

Craft is like anything else—easy to overdose on.

BRAIN FLEX

We highly recommend taking some time away from these exercises for a while at this point. It's good to let things mull and give your brain time to come at things from a fresh perspective.

Now gather your notes and your manuscript.

First, take a look at all those pages. That's all the time and energy you've dedicated to making yourself better at your passion.

Pretty impressive in and of itself.

What you're going to do now is create a hit list of all the work you've done as well as an action plan for how you can use your hard-earned knowledge going forward. Grab a blank sheet of paper and divide it in half. On the left side note each exercise and summarize what you did during the exercise. On the right side is how you're going to implement those improvements in your work on a wider scale.

When you're done, arrange the list by the order you're going to work on each item.

This isn't the easiest to hardest, or vice versa. What you're looking to do is use the summaries to figure out how to prioritize your work to begin making an impact on your voice immediately.

You can stack them however you think will be the most beneficial for you. You can work on more than one at a time as you revise. But this is the game plan. Even if you're only making a list of things to look out for in your manuscript. Don't stop here without doing this. Without this final step, this book was just a nice little read. Make it a real game changer instead.

So, Author, what is your voice?

At this point, you should be able to tell us in a sentence or two.

BRIA

My voice is a quirky, staccato voice that paces my stories quickly without feeling rushed. There is humor and comfort wrapped in truth. My voice talks over the themes of the story to spotlight them while not creating a heavy-feeling read.

JEANNIE

My voice is lyrical with subtle emotional context that gradually builds throughout the story. I employ vivid imagery to build an immersive world and create high drama.

So, tell us, what's yours?

DON'T STOP BELIEVING!

Our goal for creating this book was to both clarify as well as deconstruct our approach toward finding and developing our voices. Through that, we wanted to provide you with both the tools as well as the drive to find your own voice.

We were both blessed to have another dedicated and conscientious author working alongside us *pause for virtual hug*. The most important thing to remember is that writing is a journey. Writing is also, at its heart, a conversation. We've learned a lot in the process of putting our thoughts down into this book. The more you write, the more you think about Voice, and the more you define and discuss and deconstruct your writing and approach, the more you'll learn about your own process. Use this knowledge to inform and empower your writing.

Writing is often a lonely endeavor, but we Owls are on the same journey as you. Happy writing and keep on moving forward.

PART IX

APPENDIX A
POINTS OF VIEW

VOICE AND NARRATIVE POINT OF VIEW

There are three different types of narrative point of view, with the third commonly being broken up into three different subcategories. First person and third person limited POVs are the most commonly used in genre fiction such as romance, mystery, thriller, and scifi / fantasy. Literary fiction plays around a bit more with the less often used POVs.

- First Person
- Second Person
- Third Person Objective
- Third Person Limited (Single or Multiple)
- Third Person Omniscient

If you use an uncommon narrative POV, that's like an automatic multiplier on your uniqueness factor! But as we discussed before, a Voice that doesn't fit your genre and reader expectations may create an uphill battle.

We discuss point of view (POV) throughout the book, at one point mentioning that switching POVs may help you find your voice, but how do you know which type of narration is best suited for you? Does your choice of narration affect how you develop your Signature Voice?

We believe the tips and strategies discussed in this book apply for any type of narration, but each type of POV does have its own unique features as well as strengths and weaknesses. Depending on which approach you choose, you inherit those features. It's worthwhile to discuss the different points of view and the various benefits and challenges each one will pose.

FIRST PERSON

- The reader experiences the story directly through the narrator's eyes.
- The narrator is a character in the story, usually the protagonist.
- Uses "I" and "we."
- Examples: *The Hunger Games* trilogy by Suzanne Collins, *Bridget Jones's Diary* by Helen Fielding, *Fight Club* by Chuck Palahniuk.

First person narration sounds like the narrator is telling the story directly to the reader. The tone tends to be direct and conversational, even personal.

First person narration may employ devices like breaking the fourth wall, where the narrator appears conscious of the reader as a participant—some even literally using "dear reader" to address the reader and referring to the act of reading the story.

In first person narration, the reader only sees into the mind of the narrator and none of the other characters. The exception being when multiple first person narrators are used in a book—in which case the reader sees only one viewpoint at a time.

If you're having problems finding your natural voice, what we referred to as that first level raw voice, switching to first person narration is often a good exercise to allow you to write freely as the tone does feel more natural to many writers.

Be careful, though! Just because first person POV feels so easy to throw out on the page doesn't mean developing a powerful Signature Voice in first person is any easier. The author must still create a complex, three-dimensional narrator. A character with a unique personal history and worldview who is expected to have an effortless, natural Voice. Trying to create an authentic sounding Voice in first person for a constructed character is a huge challenge. Reading a character who is trying too hard to sound real is very jarring.

Developing a first person voice into a Signature Voice has the additional challenge of the POV being limited to a single character, including that character's individual filter on the world based on their experience. And because the tone is expected to feel even more effortless and natural than other narrative POVs, extra care has to be taken when employing the techniques we discussed about elevating and enhancing your voice.

As many readers will say, for first person POV, if the character's voice doesn't engage them, they're out. Having a strong Signature Voice is perhaps THE most important thing in first person. And there's little negotiating room there.

FIRST PERSON PERIPHERAL

A subcategory of first person is first person peripheral. In this case, the narrator is not the hero or protagonist. He or she is a bystander telling someone else's story. Two well-known examples of this are F. Scott Fitzgerald's The Great Gatsby and William Styron's Sophie's Choice.

By employing a first person narrator who is not central to the plot, the narration retains the intimate level of address, as if the reader is being taken into the narrator's confidence as he witnesses these events. The first person narration has some distance from the unfolding action and a broader view as they observe all the key players and can comment on the protagonist from the outside.

Just as with first-person direct, Signature Voice is key here, with the added challenge that the rising and falling action are not happening directly to the narrator. The narrator doesn't have access to the deep emotions and internal turmoil of the protagonists.

When we spoke of the character's, or specifically the narrator's, perspective, we mentioned four questions:
1. What is the character's emotional state?
2. Where does the character come from?
3. What is the character's view of the world?

4. How do they view their place in the world?

In first person peripheral POV, all of these elements tend to be downplayed for the narrator, while they are enhanced for his subjects. The narrator usually has less of a stake in the game than the protagonists he's describing. He also seems more interested in their journey than his own. And these features have distinct effects on the nature of the Voice employed in this POV.

This form of narration lends itself to a Voice that is objective in tone, distanced from emotion, and analytical. The first person narrator acts as a commentator with an almost journalistic approach.

That is not to say that the narrator in this POV can't experience the highs and lows of the story. These are just the characteristics of Voice that this sort of arrangement tends to create You, the author, must take it from there and mold it into your own unique Narrator with your own Signature Voice.

SECOND PERSON

- The narrator tells the story referring to the reader as "you."
- In an abstract way, the protagonist IS the reader.
- Examples: *Bright Lights, Big City* by Jay McInerney, *The Night Circus* by Erin Morgenstern.

In second person narration, the narrator is set up as an inner voice. The details of the protagonist are revealed to the reader as if the reader and the protagonist are one and the same. The narrator will tell the reader her thoughts, her motivations, and describe the things that she does and the obstacles she encounters.

The best way to explain second person is to show examples:

> *"By unclosing your eyes so suddenly, you seem to have surprised the personages of your dream in full convocation round your bed, and catch one broad glance at them before they can flit into obscurity."*
>
> —*The Haunted Mind*, Nathaniel Hawthorne

In second person POV, the identity of the protagonist is kept a mystery that is only revealed by the narrator. The voice in this narration not only takes on the quality of an inner monologue, but it also has an air of authority. Second person POV will tell you, the protagonist, everything you get to know. The reader has no choice but to accept what's handed down, even if she doesn't quite trust it—because there is no other context.

As a result, this type of Voice is one that tends to create and foster ambiguities. When developing a Signature Voice in this style, the author creates a distinct way of revealing information and directing the reader. This is a POV that begs for experimentation.

Because this POV is rare, a second person narrative voice naturally draws attention to itself. We mentioned finding a natural sweet spot and avoiding overwriting to create a Signature Voice that feels effortless. In this case, that goal may not be to have a voice that feels natural and doesn't rock the boat. Second person narration is meant to stick out.

In a Voice that's naturally attention-grabby and where all details are asked to be accepted with equal authority, the challenge then becomes how to negotiate enhancing specific elements of the Voice.

THIRD PERSON

- The reader is experiencing the story as retold by the narrator
- The narrator assumes the role of an observer
- Uses "he," "she," "them," and "they."
- Examples: Game of Thrones series by George R. R. Martin, The Princess Bride by William Goldman.

Third person is the most commonly used form of narration in fiction. Because the examples of third-person narration are so wide, it's easier to break them down into additional subcategories:

THIRD PERSON OBJECTIVE

The narrator tells the events without going into the characters' heads. Little or no interpretation or spin is put on the story elements. In terms of Voice, this is a very limiting approach in terms of Voice as emotion and motivation is only conveyed through external descriptions. Use of this narrative style in full-length stories is rare as a result, as it tends to be distancing.

THIRD PERSON LIMITED (Single POV or Multiple POV)

This is the middle ground of third person narration, and where the vast majority of third person stories fall. In limited POV, the narrator describes the emotions and inner thoughts for a single character only. The actions of other characters are filtered through the eyes of the POV character.

In addition to the use of close third person narration, it is also common to use limited third person narration for a scene or chapter, but then switch so another character takes center stage and becomes the POV character. This is second nature in the romance genre, where the heroine and hero have individual scenes which often alternate between the heroine as the POV character followed by the hero as the POV character. This allows the reader to see both sides of the story.

Though third person limited narration is potentially less intimate and less direct than first person narration, its broad approach allows for many possibilities and opportunities. Your entire Voice arsenal is at play here.

THIRD PERSON OMNISCIENT

Third person omniscient POV can be distancing and less intimate than a close third person limited narration.

In omniscient POV, the narrator is often removed from the story events, but that's not a requirement. There is a lot of potential for developing an engaging Signature Voice for an omniscient narrator, one that goes beyond what's possible with a human character voice.

If we revisit the four questions for an omniscient narrator:
What is the character's emotional state?
1. In this POV style, the narrator is all-knowing and all-seeing. The narrator has access into the mind of all the characters and describes their emotions as an outside observer because there is not necessarily a particular emphasis on identifying with any single character.
2. Where does the character come from?
3. What is the character's view of the world?
4. How do they view their place in the world?

Number one: the narrator may have emotions or not. An omniscient narration with emotional investment can definitely close the distance between the narrator and characters.

Number two: an omniscient narrator can be timeless and formless, a God's Eye, as mentioned earlier. Or there's no rule that says you can't develop some sort of backstory and origin for the narrator. The same goes for the last two. The narrator may have no opinion of the world, or they may have a large stake in it, with a goal to nurture or protect. Because an omniscient narrator is not limited by the constraints of a typical character, there are a lot of possibilities for exploring a distinctive Voice.

A recent example of omniscient POV is *The Book Thief* by Markus Zusak, wherein the omniscient narrator is the author's incarnation of Death. In the book, the narrator takes what seems to be an emotional stake or at least a great personal interest in the characters of the story. Death describes each of their emotions and even tells of future events, being all-knowing. Though the narrator is without emotion, the narration is not impassive. Death also hints at having an ongoing set of duties to perform in between the events revealed to the reader.

Given the book's mega-bestseller status, it is a prime example of how a bold and unexpected manifestation of Voice can make a book unforgettable.

Your choice of narrative POV will depend on many factors, which include genre conventions, how well the narration fits the story, and what aligns with your own Core Voice. Each form has different features for how you want to develop your Voice, but the Elements of Voice discussed throughout the book still apply to each type of POV. The type of narration you choose will undeniably affect how your Core and Signature Voices develop.

PART X

APPENDIX B

AUTHORS & EXAMPLES

- *Bet Me*, Jennifer Crusie
- The Book Thief, *Markus Zusak*
- Bright Lights, Big City, *Jay McInerney*
- The Chocolate Rose, *Laura Florand*
- Covert Evidence, *Rachel Grant*
- Game of Thrones series, George R. R. Martin
- *The Great Gatsby*, F. Scott Fitzgerald
- Kiss of a Stranger, *Lily Dane*
- The First Five Pages, *Noah Lukeman*
- The Lady or the Tiger, *Frank R. Stockton*
- The Martian, *Andy Weir*
- *Maybe This Time*, Jennifer Crusie
- Neighbors from Hell series, R.L. Mathewson
- The Night Circus, *Erin Morganstern*
- Observing the Sword Dance of a Disciple of Madame Gongsun, *Du Fu*.
- The Princess Bride, *William Goldman*
- Romancing Mr. Bridgerton, *Julia Quinn*
- Sophie's Choice, *William Styron*
- Spymaster's Lady, *Joanna Bourne*
- The Writer's Journey: Mythic Structure for Writers, *Christopher Vogler*
- You Just Don't Understand, *Deborah Tannen*

ABOUT THE OWLS

BRIA QUINLAN AND JEANNIE LIN

The Lonely Owls are not only writers — They're speakers!

We love to teach on topics ranging from Voice (obviously) to Worldbuilding and Writing Short.

And we send out a monthly mailer with articles on craft as well as guest contributions from some of our favorite authors. If you're interested in getting the Monthly Lonely Owl, sign-up at

RWA RITA award finalist and USA Today Best Seller Bria Quinlan writes Diet-Coke-Snort-Worthy Rom Coms about what it's like to be deal with junk life throws at you and still look for love. She also writes books for teens that take hard topics and make you laugh through your tears. Some people call them issue books. Some people call them romantic comedies. Bria calls them what-life-looks-like.

Her stories remind you that life is an adventure not to be ignored. For more info or to contact Bria, go to: briaquinlan.com.

USA TODAY bestselling author Jeannie Lin started writing her first book while working as a high school science teacher in South Central Los Angeles. Her stories are inspired by a mix of historical research and wuxia adventure tales. Jeannie's groundbreaking historical romances set in Tang Dynasty China have received multiple awards, including the Golden Heart for her debut novel, *Butterfly Swords*. She also writes an Opium War steampunk series and a historical erotica series under the pen name Liliana Lee.

For more info or to contact Jeannie, go to: jeannielin.com.

Made in the USA
San Bernardino, CA
02 June 2018